FIRST LIGHT ON COLORADO'S FOURTEENERS

Sunrise *from the* Summit

by Glenn Randall

FARCOUNTRY
PRESS

Colorado's Fourteeners

Peak	Elevation	Range
Mt. Elbert	14,433'	Sawatch Range
Mt. Massive	14,421'	Sawatch Range
Mt. Harvard	14,420'	Sawatch Range
Blanca Peak	14,345'	Sangre de Cristo Range
La Plata Peak	14,336'	Sawatch Range
Uncompahgre Peak	14,309'	San Juan Range
Crestone Peak	14,294'	Sangre de Cristo Range
Mt. Lincoln	14,286'	Mosquito Range
Grays Peak	14,270'	Front Range
Mt. Antero	14,269'	Sawatch Range
Torreys Peak	14,267'	Front Range
Castle Peak	14,265'	Elk Range
Quandary Peak	14,265'	Tenmile Range
Mt. Evans	14,264'	Front Range
Longs Peak	14,259'	Front Range
Mt. Wilson	14,246'	San Juan Range
Mt. Shavano	14,229'	Sawatch Range
Mt. Belford	14,197'	Sawatch Range
Crestone Needle	14,197'	Sangre de Cristo Range
Mt. Princeton	14,197'	Sawatch Range
Mt. Yale	14,196'	Sawatch Range
Mt. Bross	14,172'	Mosquito Range
Kit Carson Peak	14,165'	Sangre de Cristo Range
El Diente Peak	14,159'	San Juan Range
Maroon Peak	14,156'	Elk Range
Tabeguache Peak	14,155'	Sawatch Range
Mt. Oxford	14,153'	Sawatch Range
Mt. Sneffels	14,150'	San Juan Range
Mt. Democrat	14,148'	Mosquito Range
Capitol Peak	14,130'	Elk Range
Pikes Peak	14,110'	Front Range
Snowmass Mountain	14,092'	Elk Range
Mt. Eolus	14,083'	San Juan Range
Windom Peak	14,082'	San Juan Range
Mt. Columbia	14,073'	Sawatch Range
Missouri Mountain	14,067'	Sawatch Range
Humboldt Peak	14,064'	Sangre de Cristo Range
Mt. Bierstadt	14,060'	Front Range
Sunlight Peak	14,059'	San Juan Range
Handies Peak	14,048'	San Juan Range
Culebra Peak	14,047'	Sangre de Cristo Range
Ellingwood Point	14,042'	Sangre de Cristo Range
Mt. Lindsey	14,042'	Sangre de Cristo Range
Little Bear Peak	14,037'	Sangre de Cristo Range
Mt. Sherman	14,036'	Mosquito Range
Redcloud Peak	14,034'	San Juan Range
Pyramid Peak	14,018'	Elk Range
Wilson Peak	14,017'	San Juan Range
Wetterhorn Peak	14,015'	San Juan Range
San Luis Peak	14,014'	San Juan Range
North Maroon Peak	14,014'	Elk Range
Mt. of the Holy Cross	14,005'	Sawatch Range
Huron Peak	14,003'	Sawatch Range
Sunshine Peak	14,001'	San Juan Range

Summit elevations in this book are based on U.S. Geological Survey data as of 2014. Elevations from other sources may vary.

Table of contents photo:
Mt. Wilson at sunrise from the summit of Wilson Peak (14,017'), San Miguel Mountains, Lizard Head Wilderness, San Juan Range.

Small inset photos:
page 1: 360-degree panorama of moonset at sunrise from the summit of Sunlight Peak (14,059'), Weminuche Wilderness, San Juan Range.
page 2: 360-degree panorama of moonrise at sunset from the summit of Mt. Eolus (14,083'), San Juan Range.
page 5: Missouri Mountain and the Sawatch Range from the summit of Huron Peak (14,003'), Collegiate Peaks Wilderness, Sawatch Range.
page 25: The Rocky Mountain National Park skyline from Deer Mountain at sunrise, Front Range.
page 43: Ute Peak and Mt. Lindsey (14,042') from the summit of Blanca Peak (14,345') at sunrise, Sangre de Cristo Wilderness, Sangre de Cristo Range.
page 59: Twilight wedge over Mount of the Holy Cross (in the distance) and Traver, McNamee, and Clinton Peaks from the summit of Mt. Lincoln (14,286') at sunrise, Mosquito Range.
page 69: Ridges recede into the distance as seen from the summit of Tabeguache Peak (14,155') at sunrise, San Isabel National Forest, Sawatch Range.
page 91: 180-degree panorama at sunrise from the summit of Maroon Peak (14,156'), Maroon Bells-Snowmass Wilderness, Elk Range.
page 109: Windom Peak (14,082') panorama, San Juan Range.

ISBN: 978-1-56037-620-0

© 2015 by Farcountry Press
Photography © 2014 by Glenn Randall

CIP data is on file at the Library of Congress.

For more information about our books, write Farcountry Press, P.O. Box 5630, Helena, MT 59604; call (800) 821-3874; or visit www.farcountrypress.com.

Produced in the United States of America. Printed in China.

19   18   17   16   15   1   2   3   4   5

Table of Contents

Sunrise from the summit of Grays Peak (14,270'), near Georgetown, Front Range.

Chasing the Sun

Shooting 54 Summits

SUMMITS ARE MAGICAL PLACES. REACHING THE summit of a high peak gives me the exhilarating, humbling, and awe-inspiring experience of being a tiny speck on top of the world. To me, mountaineering is a metaphor for the human condition. It embodies in concrete form the way we reach for the sky, yet can only climb so high. In the spring of 2006, I began working on a series of images I hoped would capture these complex emotions. In my home state of Colorado, the highest peaks are the fifty-four Fourteeners—mountains that reach 14,000 feet or higher. Surely any photograph taken on the summit of a Fourteener would evoke in the viewer the same powerful emotions I experienced at that rarefied height.

But as I thought about the Fourteener summit photographs I'd seen, I realized that they were mostly rather boring. How could that be, I thought, when the experience of reaching the summit is so enthralling? Then I thought about when those

Looking north from the summit of Pikes Peak (14,110') at sunrise, near Colorado Springs, Front Range.

photos were taken: at noon, in midsummer, when the sun is as high in the sky as it will be the entire year. Most summit photos taken at that time of day show distant, hazy peaks almost lost in the white glare of the midday sun. Most good landscape photographs, by contrast, are shot at sunrise or sunset, when the light is warm and the long shadows cast by the low sun angle give the images dimension and depth. I realized I would need to seek out superb light if my summit images were going to have an impact that matched the actual experience. That meant, however, that I would somehow need to be on the summit of a 14,000-foot peak at either sunrise or sunset.

But how? Camping on the summit would be impractical and dangerous. For starters, I would need to carry food, camping gear, camera body, lenses, and tripod, plus a gallon of water, as much as 5,000 vertical feet from the trailhead to the summit. Once I got there, I would be camped atop the tallest lightning rod in the vicinity. I'd already survived several terrifying, near-miss encounters with lightning strikes while shooting above timberline but well below the summits. The risk would be even higher if I was camped on the highest point. I had no desire to fry like a mosquito caught in a bug zapper. Even if the weather was stable, I would most likely spend a sleepless night, then greet the dawn with a killer case of acute mountain sickness, the debilitating headache, nausea, and general malaise suffered by mountaineers who camp too high without allowing sufficient time for acclimatization.

I also rejected the idea of shooting sunset instead of sunrise, then descending to a camp below timberline. Although the quality of the light at sunset was potentially just as good as the light at sunrise, I'd still face an unacceptable risk from the afternoon lightning storms so typical of Colorado in the summer. There's no way to get off a Fourteener fast enough to outrun an onrushing thunderstorm. Even if I was able to stay on the summit until sunset, I would then need to

The Maroon Bells reflected in Maroon Lake, Maroon Bells-Snowmass Wilderness, Elk Range.

Glenn Randall in camp below Blanca Peak (14,345')
and Ellingwood Point (14,042'), Sangre de Cristo
Wilderness, Sangre de Cristo Range.

descend in the dark. As every seasoned mountaineer knows, the descent is actually often more dangerous than the ascent. For one, it's harder to climb down almost anything than it is to climb up. In addition, on descent, climbers are no longer fueled by the adrenaline and excitement of the ascent and sometimes let their guard down. Adding darkness to that potent cocktail of dangers would magnify the risk of an accident. And shooting sunset has another disadvantage: it would be a long, cold wait for dawn if I got off route during the descent and couldn't find my way down. If I got confused about the route heading up to shoot sunrise, I could simply pull on all my warm clothes, sit down, and wait an hour or two for the sun to come up. If I got lost on the descent, however, particularly in the winter, it could be a twelve-hour wait for light and warmth to return. Sometimes, of course, the weather is so stable that shooting sunset, then descending to a camp in the valley below, could be safe. I knew such opportunities would be rare, however.

All things considered, shooting sunrise seemed like the best option, but it was hardly an easy one. To summit a Fourteener before sunrise, starting from the road or a high camp, usually requires getting up at midnight or even earlier. The prospect of these ridiculously early starts soon led me to formulate two of Randall's Rules of Landscape Photography. The first rule is, "Sleep is for photographers who don't drink enough coffee." The second is, "Never eat breakfast before midnight. If you have to get up before midnight to do a photo shoot, eat dessert."

I had already climbed a handful of Colorado's Fourteeners, and skied off the summit of a handful more. I knew that climbing many of Colorado's Fourteeners required only a strenuous, high-altitude hike. A few Fourteeners even have constructed trails that lead all the way to the summit. All of the Fourteeners demand fitness, basic navigational skills, and the right footgear and clothing, but many don't demand advanced mountaineering techniques, at least not in the summer after the snow has melted off.

Kit Carson Peak (14,165') from the summit of Crestone Peak (14,294')
at sunrise, Sangre de Cristo Wilderness, Sangre de Cristo Range.

About seventeen of Colorado's Fourteeners, on the other hand, are semi-technical. Although experienced mountaineers don't need a rope on the standard route on any Fourteener, these seventeen peaks require basic rock-climbing skills. In addition, the routes on many of the harder peaks are "exposed," mountaineering lingo for, "if you fall, you die." These routes entail steep scrambling where a slip would have fatal consequences. No one officially tracks all fatalities on all the Fourteeners combined. Records kept by Rocky Mountain National Park, however, show that since 1884 at least fifty-eight people have died climbing 14,259-foot Longs Peak, quite possibly the deadliest Fourteener. The years 2010 and 2011 were particularly bad ones for Fourteener fatalities. Of the roughly 150,000 to 350,000 people who attempted a Fourteener each of those years, ten died.

I started technical rock climbing in 1972, when I was just fifteen years old. At the peak of my rock-climbing career, in my late twenties, I managed to lead a couple of climbs rated 5.12a, a very difficult rating even by today's elevated standards. I'd taken up ice climbing when I moved to Colorado in 1975

Missouri Mountain, Mt. Belford, Mt. Oxford, Mt. Harvard, and Mt. Columbia from
the summit of Mt. Yale (14,196'), Collegiate Peaks Wilderness, Sawatch Range.

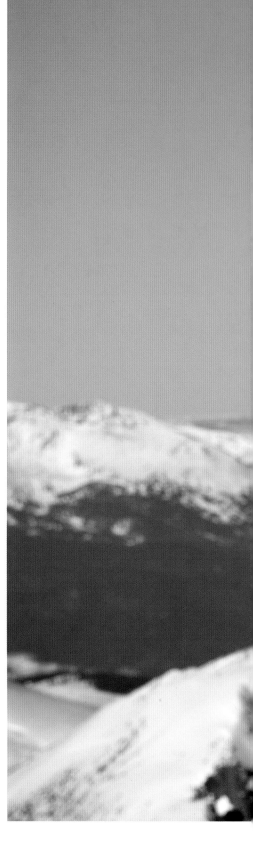

Mountain goat on the summit of Quandary Peak (14,265') in January,
near Breckenridge, Mosquito and Tenmile Ranges.

Stormy sunrise over the upper Arkansas Valley from the summit of
Mt. Columbia (14,073'), Collegiate Peaks Wilderness, Sawatch Range.

to attend the University of Colorado, and done a number of expeditions to the Alaska Range, including three ascents of Mt. McKinley, the highest and coldest peak in North America. Given my extensive background in technical climbing and mountaineering, I wasn't too worried about being unable to do the moves on any standard route on the Fourteeners. The real challenge would be finding the easiest route while navigating by headlamp at night on a peak I'd never done before. If I got off route, the difficulty

Mount of the Holy Cross (14,005') and waterfall on East Cross Creek, Holy Cross Wilderness, Sawatch Range.

of the climbing could escalate dramatically. And I knew I'd be climbing in comfortable but clunky hiking boots, not the painfully tight rock-climbing shoes I'd worn on technical climbs. Rock shoes make it much easier to use tiny nubbins as footholds, but they quickly become intolerable if worn for long periods. Carrying fifteen to twenty pounds of camera gear in addition to everything else would magnify the challenge. I was already an expert on the use of a topographic map, compass, and altimeter, since I'd written three editions of a book on the subject called *Outward Bound Map & Compass Handbook*. For many of the Fourteeners, those tools would prove to be sufficient. Five years into the project, I did begin using a high-end GPS receiver. The software accompanying the receiver allowed me to download the GPS tracks that online guidebook author Bill Middlebrook had posted on 14ers.com, convert the tracks into routes, then upload the routes to my GPS unit. These routes proved invaluable when making broad navigational decisions during the approach, but often led to more confusion than clarity when I was grappling with the intricate route-finding on the steepest terrain.

A huge project like this could obviously be defined in any number of ways. Where do I start each ascent? How do I decide when I've "done" a peak? Here's how I defined it: I started each climb where the road stopped. Two Colorado Fourteeners—Pikes Peak and Mt. Evans—have roads all the way up. For those two peaks, I drove to the top. For Fourteeners in winter,

Wilson Peak (14,017') from Wilson Mesa, near Telluride, San Juan National Forest, San Juan Range.

starting "at the end of the road" means parking where the plow stops. In some cases, such as Mt. Elbert and Mt. Yale in January and Uncompahgre Peak in March, that meant starting as low as 9,300 feet. For the remaining peaks, I drove to the end of the four-wheel-drive road—or at least as far as a stock vehicle can safely go. And while I made it easy for myself in one respect—driving to the top of Pikes Peak and Mt. Evans— I made it harder in another. In several cases, it's straightforward to climb two Fourteeners in a day. Grays and Torreys, Sunshine and Redcloud, and Oxford and Belford are three of the most obvious pairings. However, I decided that to "do" a peak meant being on the summit at either sunrise or sunset. The best photo might not be taken then, but I had to be there at one of those times to feel I'd done that peak. Climbing a second peak the same day and shooting a few photos two hours after sunrise wouldn't count.

One hallmark of my approach to landscape photography has always been careful planning. For each shoot, I started my planning by examining detailed topographic maps of the area. The view from a Fourteener can easily extend 100 miles, which means some haze is inevitable. I knew that one good strategy for minimizing the effects of haze would be to shoot at ninety degrees to the rising or setting sun. At the latitude of Colorado, the angle of sunrise (and sunset) varies by sixty degrees from summer solstice to winter solstice. For some peaks, I tried to time my shoot so that the view from the summit would include interesting peaks as I looked across the light, so that the interplay of highlights and shadows would enhance the feeling of depth. I used mapping software called The Photographer's Ephemeris to help me visualize how the light would play out across the land at different times of year. For other peaks, I chose to shoot looking directly away from the rising sun in hopes that an optical phenomenon called the twilight wedge would add a band of pink

Holy Cross Ridge from the summit of Mount of the Holy Cross
(14,005') at sunrise, Holy Cross Wilderness, Sawatch Range.

light to the sky just above a blue band representing Earth's shadow. For still other peaks, the best approach proved to be looking straight at the rising sun, dealing with the extreme difference in brightness between highlights and shadows by using high-dynamic-range software. Although the view from any Fourteener is spectacular, photographic fundamentals like an interesting foreground still matter. We naturally assume that photographs are taken looking horizontally, which means it can be hard to convey the feeling of looking down from a great height. Composing the shot to include a ridge that leads your eye from the summit on which I was standing down into the valley below turned out to be one good way of conveying the feeling of height.

For several peaks, I timed the shoot for the morning when the sun would be rising in the east just as the full moon was setting in the west. That approach was particularly appealing if the moon would be setting over some dramatic skyline. On seven peaks, I arrived early enough—or stayed late enough—to shoot the Milky Way from the summit. That meant arriving well before astronomical dawn, about two hours before sunrise in the summer, or staying until after astronomical dusk, about two hours after sunset. By shooting between astronomical dusk and dawn, when the sun is more than eighteen degrees below the horizon, I was able to work during the darkest part of the night when the stars are most vivid. The brightest part of the Milky Way appears in the constellation Sagittarius. I used Skygazer, an astronomy program, in conjunction with The Photographer's Ephemeris, to plan when and where to go to shoot the most interesting part of the Milky Way above spectacular peaks.

Above: 360-degree panorama at sunrise from the summit of North Maroon Peak (14,014'), Maroon Bells-Snowmass Wilderness, Elk Range.

For some peaks, the trailhead is high enough that it was feasible to blitz the peak in one day from the road. For seven of the first eight peaks, I worked with a 4x5 field camera, so my "daypack" weighed about forty-five pounds. Then I came to my senses and switched to high-end digital capture, shooting first with the Canon EOS 1Ds Mark III, and later the Canon 5D Mark III, which cut my summer daypack weight to around thirty pounds. For the more remote peaks, I often backpacked in to a basecamp just below timberline. My pack for a four-day shoot would typically top fifty pounds when I left the road. My basic digital kit included the camera body and three lenses: a Canon 16-35mm f/2.8 L, a Canon 50mm compact macro, and a Canon 70-200 f/4 L IS. In summer, I used a 200-series Gitzo carbon-fiber tripod with an Acratech Ultimate ballhead weighing four pounds, six ounces; in winter I needed greater stability to hold the camera steady in high winds, so I used a 300-series Gitzo carbon-fiber tripod with an Arca-Swiss Monoball ballhead weighing six pounds, twelve ounces. My winter camping gear and clothing was also much heavier than my summer kit—too heavy for me to put in a pack. I hauled most of the winter gear in a mountaineering sled, which made me feel like Scott in the Antarctic sledging toward the South Pole. The sled weighed about sixty-five pounds when I left the road on a three-day trip. I carried the camera gear in a chest pack weighing about eleven pounds, so the total gear weight was about seventy-six pounds. I used both single-row and multi-row Really Right Stuff panorama gear for the stitched panoramas.

I did my first two Sunrise from the Summit shoots on 14,433-foot Mt. Elbert, the highest mountain in Colorado, in mid-May 2006, and immediately realized that I had set myself an enormous task.

Mt. Sneffels (14,150') and a waterfall above Blue Lake, Mt. Sneffels Wilderness, San Juan Range.

My initial estimate that I could do all fifty-four Fourteeners in two years if I worked hard at it quickly proved laughable. At age forty-nine, I found it difficult to recover from a night of lost sleep, followed by a strenuous climb, while camped at altitude. Getting up at midnight and climbing just one 14,000-foot peak left me exhausted and ready for a good night's sleep in my own bed. Doing three or four peaks in a row left me feeling utterly wasted. Still, I managed to do ten summit shoots on six peaks in the summer of 2006.

I had made a good start, but in August that year I discovered that I had been hauling too big a pack for too many miles and too many years. The mild pain in my right leg that I had dismissed as a strained muscle got worse and turned into full-blown sciatica. I had herniated a disk in my lumbar spine.

For six months I fought the injury with intensive physical therapy but no surgery. By spring the pain was gone. Convinced I was cured, I worked hard to get back into shape and managed to shoot sunrise from three more Fourteeners in August 2007. I was gearing up for what I hoped would be a much more productive summer of 'Teener bagging in the spring of 2008 when disaster struck.

Slowly, insidiously, but inexorably, my sciatica came back. This time I couldn't beat it with physical therapy alone. In August 2008, I underwent surgery to remove the herniated portion of the disk. Three days later I re-herniated the disk despite my best efforts to take care of myself and had to undergo surgery once again. Recovering from surgery, then

Facing page: Milky Way over Mt. Sneffels (14,150'), Mount Sneffels Wilderness, San Juan Range.

Mt. Oxford, Mt. Belford, and Mt. Harvard from the summit of
La Plata Peak (14,336') at sunrise, San Isabel National Forest, Sawatch Range.

regaining my fitness, took six months. It was all too clear that my days of shooting sunrise from the summits of Fourteeners were numbered.

I managed to do seven shoots on six peaks in 2009, another ten shoots on ten peaks in 2010, and another ten shoots on ten peaks in 2011. When the summer of 2012 rolled around, I decided it was time to finish all the remaining hard peaks while I was still able to. I studied the routes and formulated a plan, then did three long, hard, exciting trips. By the end of the summer, I had done twelve shoots on twelve peaks, including some of the most notorious Fourteeners in the state: Pyramid Peak, Maroon Peak, Crestone Peak, Crestone Needle, Little Bear, and El Diente.

At last the end was in sight. In May 2013, I began picking off the final fourteen peaks. I knew that all the remaining peaks were high-altitude hikes; none would require scrambling. In August, I shot sunrise from the final peak, Mount of the Holy Cross, accompanied for the first time by my wife, Cora, and our two daughters, Emily, then nineteen, and Audrey, then seventeen. After seven years and sixty-seven shoots, my Sunrise from the Summit project was complete.

In the pages that follow, you'll find a unique portrait of Colorado. I've divided the book into six sections, each describing a specific mountain range. For each section, I've written an introduction that describes the character of the range, then told a few of the best stories of climbing the peaks in the range and shooting sunrise from the summit.

This book is for everyone who loves the Colorado high country, whether you've climbed every Fourteener a dozen times, like Jim Gehres, or only admired the Fourteeners from afar and wondered what the view must be like from the summit. Perhaps these photos will even evoke in you the exhilarating, humbling, and awe-inspiring feeling of being a tiny speck on top of the world. If so, then I will truly have achieved my goal.

Mountain goat on the summit of Maroon Peak (14,156'), Maroon Bells-Snowmass Wilderness, Elk Range.

Help Save the Peaks

I am hardly alone in my love of climbing Colorado's Fourteeners. On any summer weekend, the popular peaks are packed. Each year, at least 150,000 people, and perhaps as many as 350,000 people, attempt a Fourteener. More than 400 people per day, on summer weekends, climb the easiest routes on the most accessible peaks. That sheer volume of use is causing heavy wear and tear on the peaks themselves. A 14,000-foot mountain may seem indestructible, but it is not. Thousands of trampling feet can kill the tundra, which takes years to grow back. Scree slopes are actually quite susceptible to erosion inadvertently started by climbers ascending and descending the same lines over and over again. In response to the increasing damage, a group of environmental and mountaineering organizations, in partnership with the U.S. Forest Service, founded the Colorado Fourteeners Initiative in 1994. CFI is dedicated to building and maintaining sustainable routes on the highest peaks. This is an organization I actively support. I urge you to do the same. Of the hundreds of thousands of people who climb a Fourteener every year, only a tiny fraction contribute to CFI. If even ten percent of the non-members were to join, it would make the high alpine world we all love a much better place. Please join the effort. For more information, and to become a member, please visit www.14ers.org. ▲▲

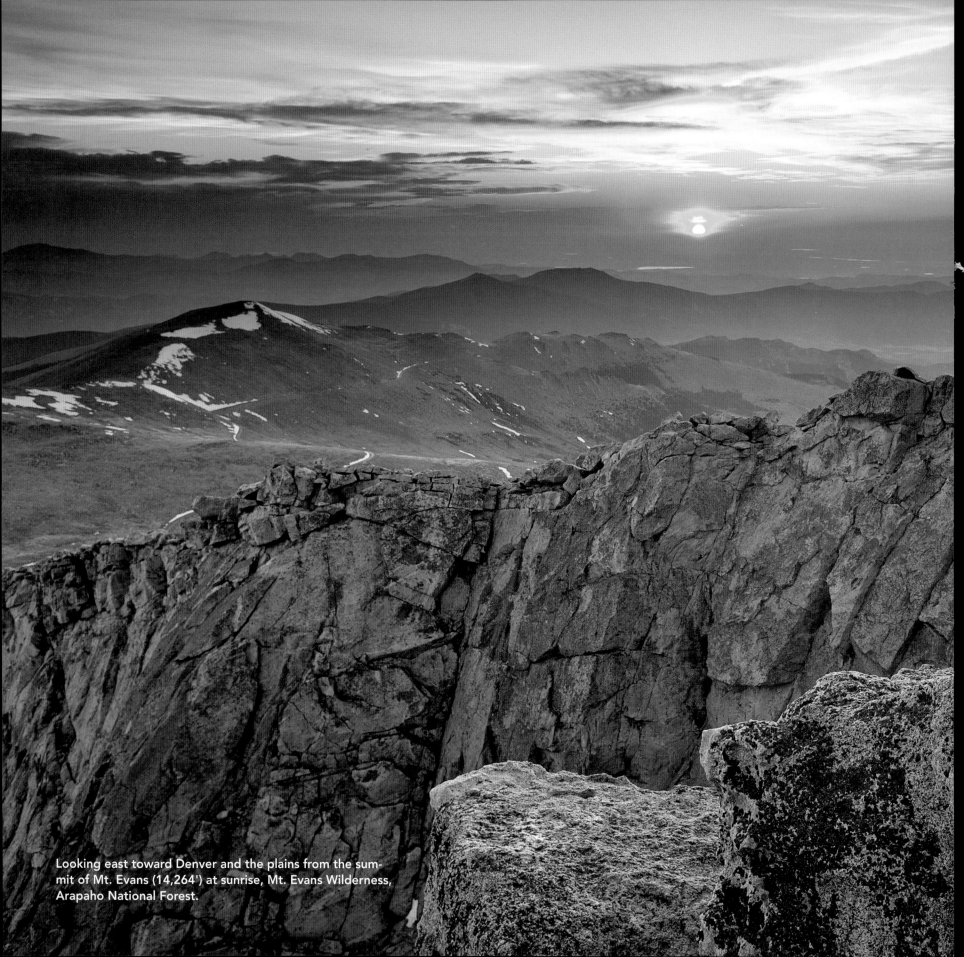

Looking east toward Denver and the plains from the summit of Mt. Evans (14,264') at sunrise, Mt. Evans Wilderness, Arapaho National Forest.

The Front Range

Grays Peak, 14,270 feet

Longs Peak, 14,259 feet

Mt. Bierstadt, 14,060 feet

Mt. Evans, 14,264 feet

Pikes Peak, 14,110 feet

Torreys Peak, 14,267 feet

LIKE MANY NEWCOMERS TO COLORADO, THE FIRST mountains I saw in the state were the peaks of the Front Range, a nearly unbroken chain of towering summits stretching from the Wyoming border south to Cañon City, a distance of 180 miles. The Front Range contains six Fourteeners, ranging from Longs Peak on the north to Pikes Peak on the south. The highest peaks rise abruptly, nearly 9,000 feet above the flat plains of eastern Colorado.

As the easternmost range in the state, the Front Range figured prominently in Colorado's early history. In 1806, a twenty-seven-year-old lieutenant named Zebulon Pike and his men set out from St. Louis, intent on exploring the southern reaches of the Louisiana Purchase and searching for the mysterious Red River. In late November, the team built a small fort on the Arkansas River near present-day Pueblo. A great mountain rose

Looking north from the summit of Pikes Peak (14,110') at sunrise, near Colorado Springs.

to the northwest, and Pike and a few companions decided to try to climb it. They struggled upward for two and a half days, but the summit was still far above them. Pike retreated, claiming the mountain was 18,000 feet high and unclimbable in winter conditions. This was the first recorded attempt to climb a Fourteener. Not for the first time, and certainly not for the last, newcomers to the mountains had underestimated the scale of Colorado's Fourteeners and the time and effort required to reach the highest points. Although Pike was unsuccessful, the peak eventually came to bear his name. Pikes Peak became a landmark for wave after wave of explorers, mountain men, and gold seekers, and for a time the entire Front Range was known as Pikes Peak country.

Fourteen years after Pike's expedition, Major Stephen Long led a team from Council Bluffs, Iowa, on the banks of the Missouri River, westward toward the Rockies. The goal was to discover the source of the Platte River. In June, the expedition reached the upper stretches of the Platte River and spotted a giant peak, which they at first took to be Pike's great mountain. Only as they explored southward and crossed the low divide between the Platte and Arkansas River drainages near present-day Sedalia (just south of Denver) did they see the peak Pike had attempted to ascend. Edwin James, the expedition's twenty-three-year-old doctor and botanist, set off with a few companions to try to scale the peak. A day and a half later, they reached the summit. This was the first recorded ascent of a Colorado Fourteener. That word "recorded" is important, since there's ample evidence that Native Americans and perhaps even a few Spanish explorers had reached the summit of several Fourteeners before 1820. In time, the first peak Long's team had spotted became known as Longs Peak.

Two of the six Fourteeners in the Front Range, Pikes Peak and Mt. Evans, have roads to the summit, which allows even flatlanders a chance to soak in the spectacular view from the roof of the Rockies.

The Sawtooth (ridge in shadow right of center) at sunset from
the summit of Mt. Bierstadt (14,060'), Mount Evans Wilderness.

Climbing three others, Bierstadt, Grays, and Torreys, requires a strenuous high-altitude hike but no technical climbing skills. Shooting sunrise from the summit primarily requires a willingness to sacrifice a night's sleep. Longs Peak, on the other hand, is a different story.

Longs Peak and I have a long history together. I moved to Boulder in 1975, ostensibly to study journalism at the University of Colorado, but in reality because a friend had told me about the incredible

Above: Longs Peak (14,259'), far left, and Forest Canyon at sunset from Trail Ridge Road, Rocky Mountain National Park.

climbing areas near Boulder. Almost immediately I began hearing tales about the highest mountain in Rocky Mountain National Park and its vertical east face, The Diamond. In the years since, I've scrambled up the Keyhole Route, the easiest route on the peak, climbed half a dozen routes on The Diamond, cramponed up Lambs Slide and the Notch Couloir in late November, and soloed Alexander's Chimney in winter. Once I even bicycled from Boulder to the Longs Peak parking lot, a distance of forty-five miles with 4,000 feet of elevation gain, then ran to the Boulderfield and scrambled up the North Face to the summit. When I told my friend Bill Briggs, an avid mountain runner himself, about that last adventure, he asked me how long it had taken.

"Eleven hours," I said. "How long did it take you?"

"I did it in nine," he replied.

"But I stopped for a meal in Allenspark," I added quickly as an excuse for my slow pace.

"So did I," he replied, with a good-natured grin.

With that kind of history, Longs Peak was naturally one of the first Fourteeners I chose for a sunrise-from-the-summit shoot. It was also one of the first Class 3 peaks I'd ever tried to solo in the dark, by headlamp, with a 4x5 field camera on my back. Class 3 is a difficulty rating used by mountaineers to describe routes requiring basic rock-climbing skills. Although experienced climbers don't generally feel a need for a rope on such routes, many Class 3 routes are exposed—which means a fall would have severe or even fatal consequences.

The weight of my pack meant there was no way I was going to reach the summit by sunrise starting from the road, so in August 2006 I got a backcountry permit and backpacked in to the Boulderfield at 12,600 feet. In a fit of excessive zeal, I shot sunset from the top of Storm King Peak that evening, got to bed at 9:45 p.m. and was hiking again by 2 a.m. To my surprise, I summited in just over two and a half hours with no major route-finding mistakes. I was so early I had an hour to wait until there was enough light to see where to set up my camera. When the sunrise light faded, I descended to the Boulderfield, packed up my camp, and staggered back down the trail carrying my seventy-five-pound load of large-format camera and camping gear. I reached the road feeling completely wrung out. Within a few weeks after the trip, the nagging

Chasm Lake and Longs Peak (14,259')
in mid-July after a heavy snow year,
Rocky Mountain National Park.

Right: Longs Peak (14,259') from the
Rock Cut, Rocky Mountain National Park.

Looking northwest toward Grays and Torreys Peaks from the summit of
Mt. Evans (14,264'), Mt. Evans Wilderness, Arapaho National Forest.

"pulled muscle" in my hip that had been plaguing me since my Castle Peak shoot earlier in the year turned into shooting pains down my right leg caused by the herniated disc in my lumbar spine. All photography plans went on the shelf, and I began my first six-month battle with debilitating sciatica.

That experience taught me (again) the folly of a 136-pound guy carrying a 75-pound pack. It also taught me that August is not the ideal time of year. With no snow left on the peaks, the blue-gray shadowed rock of one mountain blends in almost perfectly with the blue-gray rock of the next, so there's very little separation of tones. It's almost like the peaks are wearing camouflage.

A better time to shoot, I decided, was early June, when the lingering remnants of the winter snowpack would delineate the gullies and ridges of the dramatic peaks to the west of Longs. In 2010, four years after my first sunrise shoot on Longs, I laid plans to return.

As photogenic as I expected it to be, the snow introduced a new problem: finding my way up the snow-covered Class 3 rock of the Keyhole Route in the dark. In August, the entire route had been a frolic up dry rock; in early June, it would be a different climb entirely. A ranger at the Longs Peak Ranger Station who'd climbed the peak just a few days before told me he'd put on his crampons at the Keyhole, where the scrambling begins, and worn them all the way to the summit.

The climb itself posed a significant challenge; the weather complicated matters still further. Powerful storms and high winds frequently rake Longs Peak in early June. I had switched to digital camera gear in 2008, which lightened my pack considerably, but it still wasn't feasible for me to blitz the peak in a day from Boulder. I decided to camp in the

Glenn Randall on the summit of Mt. Bierstadt (14,060'), Grays and Torreys Peaks behind, Mount Evans Wilderness.

Boulderfield, a rocky valley far above timberline on a notoriously windy mountain. I'd already had one tent destroyed by wind in the middle of the night in the Boulderfield many years before, and I wasn't eager to repeat the experience.

I packed for an overnight shoot and started watching the weather carefully. On Friday evening, June 4, the forecast for the following two days called for partly cloudy skies with winds gusting to twenty-two miles per hour—breezy, but hardly tent-threatening. On Saturday morning, I started driving to the Longs Peak Ranger Station. As I topped the hill just east of Allenspark, powerful gusts began buffeting my Toyota 4Runner. Swirling plumes of sand snaked across the road ahead. At the ranger station I got an updated forecast. A glance told the tale: gusts to sixty-five miles per hour were now forecast for 13,000 feet. Berating myself for not checking the forecast one last time before leaving home, I drove back to Boulder to wait.

The next opportunity came just twenty-four hours later, with gusts to thirty miles per hour predicted for Sunday and Sunday night, climbing to forty-six miles per hour Monday afternoon—unpleasant but survivable.

After five hours of strenuous, windy hiking, I reached the Boulderfield and camped. The twin alarms inside my ski hat sounded their clarion call at 12:30 a.m. In less than an hour, I was climbing toward the summit. I lost the route briefly just past the Keyhole, then found it again. Fortunately, there had been enough traffic on the route that I could follow tracks in the snow in many places. Before the trip, I had been intimidated by the short but steep granite dihedral at the top of the Trough that leads to the beginning of the Narrows. It had been years since I'd climbed rock in crampons. But as so often happens, the fears that beset me when I'm lying awake at midnight proved to be exaggerated. My crampon's front points gripped securely on the small but solid holds, and the dihedral turned out to be easy.

Winter sunrise on Longs Peak (14,259') from Chasm Lake, Rocky Mountain National Park.

Longs Peak (14,259') from the western flank of Twin Sisters at sunrise, Rocky Mountain National Park.

Left: Longs Peak (14,259') from an aspen grove on the western flank of Twin Sisters in summer, Rocky Mountain National Park.

As I began traversing the Narrows at about 4 a.m., a flash of light glinted off my glasses. Lightning? At this ungodly hour? If so, where? To the west, where any storm would be heading in my direction? I was already at 14,000 feet, just a few hundred feet below the summit, but with the most difficult scrambling still above me. I turned and scanned the western horizon. No dark clouds were visible against the stars, and I heard no thunder. I continued upward, nervously. Several more flashes sparked more fear, but still I heard no thunder. I topped out at 4:30 a.m. and for the first time was able to look east. An enormous thunderhead over the plains was spitting cloud-to-ground lightning. Fortunately, the storm was heading east, away from the mountains. I shed my crampons, set up the tripod, and grabbed a few twenty-second exposures of the dark cloud silhouetted against the dawn glow. Then I walked over to the extreme southwestern corner of the summit plateau. This was the image I'd really come for: a 200-degree panorama of the Continental Divide, from the Indian Peaks to the south to the Mummy Range to the north. Longs Peak sits just east of the main crest of its range, making it an ideal vantage point for a big panorama (see following page).

As I knew it would be, the wind was screaming up the western flank of Longs and blasting over the edge of the summit plateau. I set up atop a precarious granite rib projecting out over the void in the full strength of the wind. On the hike to the Boulderfield, I'd cursed the weight of my big carbon-fiber Gitzo tripod, Arca-Swiss B1 ballhead, and Really Right Stuff pano-head. Now I was thankful I'd brought such a rock-solid combination. Although murky skies to the east blocked any colorful light at the moment of sunrise, I was blessed with interesting cirrus clouds to the west. When the sun found a thin spot in the clouds a few minutes after sunrise, the soft, warm beam put texturing light on the peaks north and south of Longs' shadow without generating excessive contrast. After shooting five panorama sequences, I headed down, reminding myself that tripping over my crampons could easily be a fatal mistake. Two hours later, I reached my campsite and was relieved to find my tent still standing. After some freeze-dried eggs and a quick siesta, I packed up and headed home, eager to escape the Boulderfield before the wind began gusting even harder. Longs Peak had tolerated my presence only grudgingly, and I didn't want to try its patience. ▲▲

Following pages: 200-degree panorama from the summit of Longs Peak (14,259'), Rocky Mountain National Park, Colorado. From left to right, the panorama extends from the Indian Peaks Wilderness to the south to the Mummy Range to the north.

The Milky Way over Longs Peak (14,259')
from the Emerald Lake Trail after an April
snowstorm, Rocky Mountain National Park.

Crestone Needle (14,197') and the southern peaks of the Sangre de Cristo Range from the summit of Crestone Peak (14,294') at sunrise, Sangre de Cristo Wilderness.

The Sangre de Cristo Range

Blanca Peak, 14,345 feet

Crestone Needle, 14,197 feet

Crestone Peak, 14,294 feet

Culebra Peak, 14,047 feet

Ellingwood Point, 14,042 feet

Humboldt Peak, 14,064 feet

Kit Carson Peak, 14,165 feet

Little Bear Peak, 14,037 feet

Mt. Lindsey, 14,042 feet

BY 1916, ONLY THREE FOURTEENERS IN COLORADO had never been climbed: Kit Carson, Crestone Peak, and Crestone Needle. All are in the Sangre de Cristo Range, and that simple fact tells you a lot about the character of those peaks. The Sangres, as they are known to climbers, are an extraordinary chain of mountains that tower more than 6,000 feet above the Wet Valley to the east and the San Luis Valley to the west. The range is long—about 120 miles from Salida on the north to the New Mexico border on the south—but only 10 or 12 miles wide through much of its length. Nine Fourteeners form the climax of the range, concentrated in two groups. The Crestone group includes Kit Carson, Crestone Peak, Crestone Needle, and Humboldt Peak; the Blanca massif includes Blanca Peak, Ellingwood Point, Little Bear, and Mt. Lindsey. In between those two groups lies Great Sand Dunes National Park, home to the highest sand dunes in North America. Culebra Peak, the only Fourteener in Colorado that is entirely privately owned, rises well to the south of the Blanca massif, just a few miles north of the New Mexico state line. In Colorado, only the view of the Sneffels Range as you drive south from Montrose toward Ridgway is comparable in the way dramatic peaks rise so abruptly from broad, gentle valleys.

The history of mountaineering in the Sangres, and in Colorado, is inextricably intertwined with the triumphant and tragic story of Albert Ellingwood, one of the sport's most daring and prolific pioneers. Ellingwood was born in Iowa on June 22, 1887, but moved to Colorado to attend high school and college. He won a Rhodes scholarship in 1910 and studied for three years in Oxford, England, earning a degree in civil law. While there, he became an enthusiastic climber and learned the rudiments of using a rope to protect himself and his partners on difficult rock climbs. When he returned to the United States, he brought these new techniques with him and soon put them to good use.

In July 1916, he organized an expedition to attempt the last three unclimbed Fourteeners in the state. In an era when it was considered scandalous for a woman to wear pants, he chose seven women as his climbing partners. Among them was Eleanor Davis, a talented athlete who taught physical education at Colorado College, the same institution in Colorado Springs where Ellingwood taught political science. The party hired burros to help carry their gear to a basecamp near Willow Lake on the west side of the range, then tackled Kit Carson via the northwest ridge. When they reached the sub-peak on the ridge now called Challenger Point, they could see that

14,197-foot Crestone Needle after an April snowstorm, Sangre de Cristo Wilderness.

Right: Challenger Point (14,080') and Kit Carson Peak (14,165'), Sangre de Cristo Range.

Crestone Needle (14,197') and Crestone Peak (14,294') at sunrise from
the summit ridge of Humboldt Peak (14,064'), Sangre de Cristo Wilderness.

continuing on the northwest ridge to the summit was probably impossible. They could also see a narrow, steeply sloping ledge slashing across the southwest face of the peak that is now called Kit Carson Avenue. The ledge led to a small notch in the south ridge. Unlike most climbers today, Ellingwood and his team climbed straight up the steep, knobby wall that leads from the notch to the summit. Today, most climbers follow the ledge beyond the notch to much easier terrain on the southeast flank of the peak that leads circuitously to the summit.

After moving camp over to the Spanish Creek drainage, Ellingwood, Davis, Frances "Bee" Rogers, and Jo Deutchbein tackled the formidable northeast buttress of Crestone Peak. Ellingwood led, belaying the rest of the team as necessary on the more difficult sections. At 1 p.m., the team reached Crestone Peak's western summit. Concluding wrongly that the eastern summit was actually higher, the team climbed that as well.

Now only one Fourteener in the state was left unclimbed: Crestone Needle, just half a mile to the southeast. The ridge between Crestone Peak and Crestone Needle looked formidable, however, with a series of near-vertical towers on the ridge that would have to be circumvented, and then a final steep, smooth pitch to the summit. Rogers and Deutchbein elected to descend the south face of Crestone Peak, then circle around the western flank of the mountain back to their camp in Spanish Creek—in itself a significant accomplishment, since their route led across completely unknown terrain.

Ellingwood and Davis, meanwhile, started across the traverse, staying below the most precipitous pinnacles, then finding a way up the crux pitch to the summit. The last unclimbed Fourteener in the state, a peak that many had thought was unclimbable, had seen its first ascent. It was already 5 p.m., and

Crestone Needle (14,197') reflected in South Colony Lake at sunrise, Sangre de Cristo Wilderness.

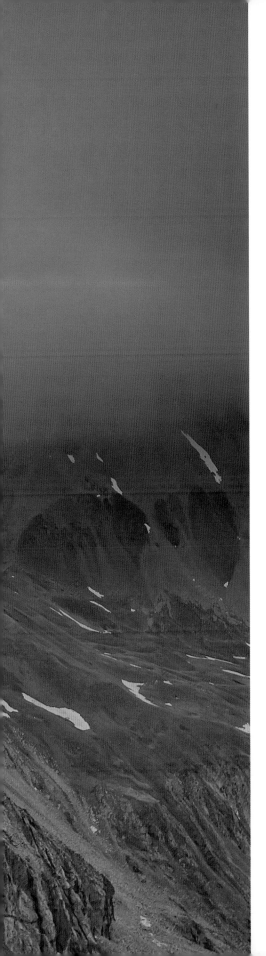

Left: Mist engulfs Ute Peak and Mt. Lindsey (14,042'), seen from the summit of Blanca Peak (14,345'), Sangre de Cristo Wilderness.

they still had to figure out how to descend the intricate maze of chimneys, gullies, ribs, and cliffs that forms the south flank of Crestone Needle. Once they reached Broken Hand Pass, they dropped down into the South Colony Lake drainage. As darkness fell, they lit a candle lantern, only to have the persistent wind snuff it out. After climbing over Bear's Playground, as the saddle between Crestone Peak and Humboldt Peak is known today, they headed down to their campsite, finally reaching their tent at 11:15 p.m.

Ellingwood went on to make many other first ascents and early repeat ascents in Colorado and Wyoming, including the first ascent in 1925 of the awesome northeast ridge of Crestone Needle, which is now known as Ellingwood Arête. His life was cut short in 1934, when he died at age forty-six of complications following surgery. Davis, on the other hand, remained active until well into her nineties and finally died at age 107 in 1994.

I knew I was following in the footsteps of giants when I began my own adventures in the Sangres. Shooting sunrise from the summit proved to be a challenge on almost every Fourteener in the range. On Kit Carson, I underestimated how long it would take to use crampons and an ice ax to traverse the steep, rock-hard snow still covering Kit Carson Avenue in early June. With a 1,400-foot cliff immediately below me, slipping was not an option. I sprinted up the final slabs and reached the summit just three minutes before the sun crested the horizon. On Blanca Peak, I left camp at 1 a.m. under clear, starry skies but was engulfed in fog soon after reaching the summit. A thunderstorm appeared to be imminent, and I fled from the summit just minutes after an eerie sunrise. Little Bear lived up to its reputation as the nastiest Fourteener in the state. The crux slabs in the Hourglass Couloir were coated with a thin, almost invisible sheet of ice called verglas. The ice was too thin to climb with crampons and too thick to easily chip away, so I was forced to climb dry but much more difficult rock nearby. On Mt. Lindsey I had just launched myself onto the 4th-class crux of the northwest ridge when my headlamp battery suddenly died. I was standing on a six-inch-wide ledge on a moonless night. The ledge was too small to take off my pack and retrieve a spare battery, and it was too dark to climb back down to a larger ledge without some kind of light. Fortunately, I had thought ahead enough to stash a spare battery and a tiny backup headlamp in a pouch attached to my pack's shoulder straps. I was able to replace the battery in my main headlamp, finish the crux moves, then climb to the summit, arriving in time to witness an ominous sunrise as smoke from the numerous wildfires burning across Colorado filled the air.

Quite possibly the most exciting adventures, however, were on Crestone Peak and Crestone Needle. I first climbed Crestone Needle in April 1991 to photograph Lou Dawson making the second ski descent. (No, I did not ski it myself. I too had steel under my feet, but it was in the form of crampons, not ski edges.) Now, more than twenty years later, it was time to return to try to photograph sunrise from the summit.

After a week of recovery from my first Sangres expedition of 2012, in which I had climbed Kit Carson, Blanca, Little Bear, and Ellingwood, I headed down the east side of the range to the South Colony Lakes trailhead and backpacked in several miles to a campsite just below the lake. It had been a low snow year, but I still brought crampons and an ice ax to deal with the snowfields below Broken Hand Pass. I intended to climb the south face route that Ellingwood and Davis had descended. Although I would be climbing at night, which would surely magnify the difficulty of the route-finding, I was armed with a device that would have astonished Ellingwood: a GPS receiver loaded with a route created by Bill Middlebrook of 14ers.com.

Looking north down the Huerfano Valley from the summit of
Ellingwood Point (14,042') at sunset, Sangre de Cristo Wilderness.

Looking north from the summit of Ellingwood Point (14,042')
at sunset, Sangre de Cristo Wilderness.

Right: Little Bear Peak (14,037'), Blanca Peak (14,345'), and Ellingwood Point (14,042') from the summit of Mt. Lindsey (14,042') at sunrise, Sangre de Cristo Wilderness.

As usual for the harder peaks, I was on the trail a few minutes after midnight. The Rocky Mountain Field Institute has built a steep but solid trail to a point several hundred vertical feet below Broken Hand Pass. After a few awkward moves past a giant chockstone, with one foot on rock and one foot on snow and ice, I scrambled up the final gritty gully to the pass, then on up the narrow but well-defined trail leading to the beginning of the more serious scrambling. So far, so good. With the GPS pointing me in the right direction, I found my way into the first of the two major gullies on the south face, known to climbers as the east gully. The route-finding crux, I knew, was finding the correct exit from the east gully and entrance into the west gully. If I missed that crucial traverse, the climbing would get much harder.

With the help of the GPS, I found the exit. The climbing was steep, sustained, and exposed, but the rock was solid, and I summited an hour before dawn. After photographing the spectacular view of Crestone Peak at sunrise, I turned my attention to the descent.

Almost immediately I realized why so many mountaineers had reached the summit of Crestone Needle, then gotten lost heading down. Nothing looked familiar. And why should it? It had been twenty years since I had seen it in daylight. Two sharp ridges, both with cairns, seemed to lead in the right direction. I started down the right-hand of the two, thinking it would lead to the west gully, and immediately thought, "This is dangerous." I turned the GPS back on and pointed it toward the waypoint I'd created at the top of the west gully. Finally I spotted the gully entrance. I down-climbed a steep wall that I felt sure I hadn't climbed on the way up and reached the top of the gully. Surely everything now would be straightforward. I had set a second waypoint at the beginning of the traverse from the west gully into the east gully. But as I descended the west gully and got close to that waypoint, I saw an easy side gully leading up to the crest of the rib between the two gullies. It didn't look familiar, but then again, nothing did. I climbed up to the crest of the rib and peered over. No cairns. I descended back into the west gully and tried a traverse line leading toward the east gully. It proved to be way too steep and difficult, and I retreated. Where was the traverse? The GPS told me it should be right there. Descending still farther down the west gully looked ugly. Finally, I climbed back up the easy side gully, crossed the rib, and headed down the east gully.

Soon I realized that I had traversed too high. I was still above the crux headwall in the east gully—a crux that the crucial traverse would have allowed me to avoid. The gully narrowed and steepened

into a chimney with gritty walls. Just as I was about to climb back up the east gully, traverse into the west gully, and try for the third time to find the correct exit, I spotted a cairn leading me out of the throat of the east gully onto steep, smooth slabs studded with conglomerate stones the size of grapefruit. The climbing was 4th class but on solid rock. I picked my way down carefully and finally regained the standard route. After one more minor route-finding error, I finally reached camp four hours after leaving the summit, deeply impressed and humbled by Ellingwood and Davis's accomplishment in 1916.

There is no easy approach to Crestone Peak, the next mountain on my itinerary. Approaching from my campsite near South Colony Lake would require climbing to Broken Hand Pass at nearly 13,000 feet, then descending 600 vertical feet to Cottonwood Lake. From there, the route climbs a steep gully called the Red Couloir that splits the south face of Crestone Peak. Finding the entrance to the gully, which begins

Above: 220-degree panorama of the Sangre de Cristo Range at sunrise in late April from the summit ridge of Humboldt Peak (14,064'), Sangre de Cristo Wilderness, Colorado. The two prominent rocky peaks in the center are Crestone Needle (left, 14,197') and Crestone Peak (14,294').

just above a cliff, sounded like the only route-finding challenge. I would need to find my way around that cliff to the right in the dark, then find the entrance to a narrow bench that would lead me back to the base of the Red Couloir. If I missed that entrance, I would be confronted with impassable cliffs.

I planned to start the day after climbing Crestone Needle with a sunrise shoot at South Colony Lake, then move camp over Broken Hand Pass to Cottonwood Lake. When I got up at 4:30 a.m., I could tell immediately there was much more moisture in the air than there had been when I went to bed. The sky was overcast as I hiked by headlamp up to the edge of South Colony Lake. As the gloom lightened, I could see that the tip of Crestone Needle was shrouded in mist. Catching up on lost sleep suddenly seemed like a much better idea than wasting time standing around on a sodden, gray morning. I resisted the urge to hurry back to my warm sleeping bag and waited. Then, to my surprise, the rising sun found

a hole in the mist and cast a band of warm light across the dramatic cliffs of Crestone Needle, which was reflected in South Colony Lake. I held my breath and started shooting, praying the wind would stay calm to preserve the reflection. When the light show faded, I returned to camp, packed up, and headed up Broken Hand Pass. By the time I arrived at Cottonwood Lake, all traces of mist had vanished and the day had become sunny and hot. I turned in early, expecting a clear sunrise the next day.

The Rocky Mountain Field Institute has built a solid trail to the base of the Red Couloir. I had hiked far enough up the trail the previous day to get a look at what I needed to do, and I thought the route-finding would be straightforward. But I lost the trail in the dark in a big talus field. The GPS route I had downloaded from 14ers.com wasn't helpful; it kept pointing me straight up a cliff band. If I was below the entrance to the bench, I should go up and right; if I was already above it, I should go down and left. After wasting several precious minutes wandering around in the dark, I finally tackled the cliff band head on and soon got back on route.

From there, the route-finding was straightforward. After dealing with the crux—some steep slabs near the bottom of the couloir—the difficulty eased. I was already 1,000 feet up the gully when the stars suddenly vanished. Mist welled up from the abyss below and swallowed me. My headlamp had been throwing a usable shaft of light for nearly 100 yards. Now it began reflecting off the mist. It was like driving on a foggy night with your high beams on. Suddenly I could barely see twenty feet.

I debated descending but remembered how quickly the fog had dissipated yesterday morning after the sun rose. I continued upward, cautiously, as the fog ebbed and flowed. A fantastic scene greeted me on the summit as the sun rose. Waves of fog were rolling up the valleys to the west, cresting the jagged ridges all around me, then breaking like waves. Warm light from the rising sun shone through the fog and kissed the crests of the waves. I photographed in every direction until the light grew harsh and the fog dissipated, then headed down. After breaking camp, I hiked energetically back to Broken Hand Pass, fueled by the excitement of the unique scenes I'd just witnessed. A strong west wind was building as I crested the pass, then headed down the east side. By the time I reached a campsite below South Colony Lake, the wind was screaming even down in the trees. After a restless night spent lying awake wondering if the tent poles would break in the next gust, I packed up and headed for Mt. Lindsey, the last of the hard Sangre Fourteeners. ▲▲

Wheeler Mountain, Fletcher Mountain, and Quandary Peak (14,265')
from the summit of Mt. Democrat (14,148') at sunset, Mosquito Range.

The Mosquito and Tenmile Ranges

Mt. Bross, 14,172 feet
Mt. Democrat, 14,148 feet
Mt. Lincoln, 14,286 feet
Mt. Sherman, 14,036 feet
Quandary Peak, 14,265 feet

P EOPLE CLIMB MOUNTAINS FOR MANY REASONS, some overt and some hidden even from themselves. Native Americans were probably the first people to wander up to the broad, accessible summits of the five Fourteeners in the Mosquito and Tenmile Ranges near Breckenridge, motivated perhaps by a desire to learn more about their territory or by simple curiosity. The motivations of the miners who followed them and staked claims as high as 14,172 feet, on the very summit of Mt. Bross, are clearer. Gold and silver were the obvious lures, but the romance of life on the frontier undoubtedly played a role.

For some, the summits of the Mosquito Range have been the setting for romance of a different sort. Not long after I finished

Left: Pikes Peak (14,110') rises above the fog blanketing South Park at sunrise as seen from the summit of Mt. Lincoln (14,286'), Mosquito Range.

my Sunrise from the Summit project, I received an order for a print of *Sunset from Mt. Democrat.* A husband planned to give it to his wife as a present. He and his wife had exchanged their wedding vows on the summit. They plan to climb all the Fourteeners together.

Not long afterwards, a woman ordered a print of *Sunrise from Mt. Sherman.* When I asked her what attracted her to this particular Fourteener, she replied, "I haven't been to Mt. Sherman, but the love of my life climbed to the top and it's where he sat and realized that I too am the greatest love of his life. I was thrilled to find something that we can both look at and know the path that brought us together."

My own romance with these ranges began in the late 1980s, when I learned that Quandary Peak offers some of the best spring ski-mountaineering in the state. Unlike most Fourteeners, which are too rocky, steep, and windblown to hold skiable snow, Quandary Peak offers a spectacular run down its east flank that starts on the very summit. Over the years, I skied Quandary Peak several times, but my first effort to shoot sunrise from the summit, in May 2008, ended in a miserable failure when I arrived late on the summit after an exhausting struggle with deep spring snow. The onset of my second battle with sciatica a few weeks later prevented a repeat attempt.

By the summer of 2009, my back was healthy enough to allow me to shoot sunrise from the summits of four peaks in the San Juans. Then October arrived, and with it the first fall storms, which coated the high peaks with snow. The weather forecast the morning of October 16, however, called for a strong ridge of high pressure to move in that day, and I began wondering if I could bag another Fourteener or two before all the access roads were closed by snow. Climbing Fourteeners in true winter conditions is much more difficult than in summer for many reasons, but one of the biggest is difficult access. Summer trailheads usually lie between 10,000 and 11,000 feet; in winter, the roads leading to the summer trailheads are blocked by snow, adding many miles and thousands of feet of elevation gain to the approach.

I had never done Mt. Lincoln and Mt. Democrat, in the Mosquito Range just south of Hoosier Pass. Kite Lake, the summer trailhead, lies at 12,000 feet—very high for a Fourteener trailhead. Suddenly it occurred to me that if the road was still open all the way to Kite Lake, and if I hurried, I might be able to pack up that morning, drive to the trailhead, climb Mt. Democrat that afternoon and shoot sunset from the summit, descend in the dark to Kite Lake, sleep in my truck for a few hours, then climb Mt. Lincoln in the dark and shoot sunrise from its summit.

I called the Forest Service and was told that the recent storms had probably made it very difficult to drive to Kite Lake. The ranger hadn't checked the road in person, however, so I decided to see for myself. To my delight, the road was almost dry all the way to the trailhead. As I started hiking up the mountain around 3 p.m., I encountered two climbers who had arrived the day before and been forced to park several miles down the road by snow. In one day, enough snow had melted to reopen the road. By pure luck, my timing had been perfect.

A well-defined trail leads to the summit of Mt. Democrat, so the climb presented no technical challenges. Snow on the trail made the footing slippery, but the biggest problem was the wind, which at one point gusted to fifty miles per hour and nearly knocked me down. Fortunately, the wind had eased by the time I summited an hour before sunset. Although nervous about descending in the dark, I forced myself to keep shooting until the last pink light had faded from the sky, then stowed my gear in haste and

Above: 260-degree panorama at sunrise in January from the summit of Quandary Peak (14,265'), Tenmile Range, near Breckenridge.

bolted for the truck over 2,000 feet below. Wind-drifted snow had already covered my tracks just below the summit, but I was able to spot the trail again lower down and stay on route.

By the time I reached my truck an hour and a quarter later, I had developed a headache and a rather queasy stomach. I knew I needed to eat to refuel for my effort on Mt. Lincoln just a few hours away, but I couldn't force down any food. Finally I wriggled into my sleeping bag with the alarm set for 2:30 a.m., hoping some sleep would make me feel better. I thought it quite likely, however, that I would wake up still feeling sick, turn off the alarm, and go back to sleep. My luck, it seemed, might have run out.

My alarm yanked me out of a restless sleep at 2:30 a.m. My headache was gone. I started up the trail an hour later. My shoot coincided with the new moon, and the night seemed unbelievably dark, with laser-bright stars. The wind, thankfully, had eased to a gentle, intermittent breeze. I topped Mt. Cameron (a bump on the long ridge leading to Mt. Lincoln) just as a faint glow began along the eastern horizon and summited

Mt. Lincoln half an hour before sunrise. The high-altitude air was very clear, with almost no haze. A richly colored twilight wedge developed over Mount of the Holy Cross, so I shot it first, then photographed Pikes Peak rising out of the fog filling South Park 4,000 feet below. When I finished shooting the best light, I hiked out and drove home, delighted that I'd pulled off a plan that seemed doomed to fail at least twice. Total time, front door to front door: twenty-five hours and fifteen minutes. It had seemed much longer.

After my success on Democrat and Lincoln, I began wondering if it was possible to shoot sunrise from the summit of a Fourteener in winter. I knew that Quandary was a likely candidate. Map study after my fiasco the year before had shown that the best time of year for a rematch was probably winter, when the rising sun would put texturing side light on the dramatic peaks north of Quandary, rather than spring.

Climb a Fourteener in the dark and shoot sunrise from the summit in the depths of winter? Was I nuts? I hadn't climbed a Fourteener in winter in thirty years. True, Quandary would be a lot easier than the Notch Couloir on Longs Peak, but I wasn't twenty-two anymore, either. I imagined myself breaking trail in bottomless depth hoar while I dragged my sled over deadfall on my way to a high camp at 11,600 feet, then imagined getting up at 1 a.m. on a bitterly cold, windy night and struggling to keep my face from becoming frostbit as I fought my way to the summit in gale-force winds. Feeling thoroughly intimidated, I waited for a good weather window. When it arrived, in January 2010, I packed up, drove to the trailhead, and found a surprise.

The parking lot was full. A wide, packed trail led up the snow-covered road leading to the summer trailhead. I hitched up my sled and started upward. Soon I met the first of a series of climbers descending from the summit. "Forty people summited Quandary today," he told me. "There was something about climbing Quandary today on 14ers.com. I guess the guy who runs the website organizes this every year." I continued upward in the warm sunshine, following the well-packed summer trail, and reached my high camp in just an hour and a half.

"Surely it can't be this easy," I thought. Bitterly mindful of my tardy arrival on the summit on my first attempt, I set my alarm for 1 a.m., determined this time to summit at least half an hour before sunrise.

A packed trail led me all the way to the summit the next morning—or maybe I should say, that night, since I arrived on the summit an hour and forty-five minutes before sunrise when it was still thoroughly dark. I whiled away the time before sunrise experimenting with star field photographs, discovering too

late that I had ruined all of them by not setting the camera properly in the dark, then pulled myself together when dawn light began to spread across the sky. Now I set up to shoot a 260-degree panorama, starting with Mt. Lincoln to the south, sweeping past the Maroon Bells, Mount of the Holy Cross, and Pacific Peak, and ending with the valley of the Blue River leading north toward Breckenridge.

When I finished photographing this marvelous display of natural light, I packed up and got ready to descend. Just as I was about to hoist my pack, I heard a clattering noise behind me. Slightly annoyed that my solitude had been disturbed by what I assumed was the first of a horde of climbers, I turned and saw three mountain goats stroll casually across the summit and along the summit ridge. Frantically, I dug my camera gear back out of my pack and tried to get a photo. What on earth were three mountain goats doing on the summit of a 14,000-foot peak in January? They seemed perfectly at home in their three-inch-thick fur coats. After locating some flat, snow-free rocks, they settled down for a nap. I was ready for a nap too, but fought to stay awake so as not to miss the moment when they awoke. After half an hour, the goats got up, posed obligingly for photos with Mount of the Holy Cross in the background, then descended a steep gully on the south face. I descended too, down the east ridge, pausing at 13,000 feet to remove gloves and strip down to long johns. I'd seen worse weather on Quandary in May than on this January day when fortune seemed to smile at every turn. ▲▲

South Park and the valley of Buckskin Creek from the summit
of Mt. Democrat (14,148') at sunset, Mosquito Range.

Looking south-southwest at sunrise along the crest of the Mosquito Range toward
Mt. Sherman (14,056') from the summit of Mt. Lincoln (14,286'), Mosquito Range.

A sea of fog fills the valley of the Arkansas River as seen from the summit of Mt. Princeton (14,197') at sunrise, San Isabel National Forest.

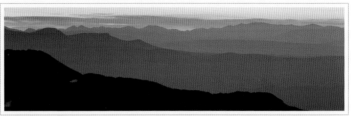

The Sawatch Range

Huron Peak, 14,003 feet
La Plata Peak, 14,336 feet
Missouri Mountain, 14,067 feet
Mount of the Holy Cross, 14,005 feet
Mt. Antero, 14,269 feet
Mt. Belford, 14,197 feet
Mt. Columbia, 14,073 feet
Mt. Elbert, 14,433 feet
Mt. Harvard, 14,420 feet
Mt. Massive, 14,421 feet
Mt. Oxford, 14,153 feet
Mt. Princeton, 14,197 feet
Mt. Shavano, 14,229 feet
Mt. Yale, 14,196 feet
Tabeguache Peak, 14,155 feet

MENTION "MOUNTAINEERING" TO MOST PEOPLE, and they immediately envision Matterhorn-like peaks where the chief danger faced by climbers is a fatal fall from unimaginable heights. They don't picture the gentle giants of Colorado's Sawatch Range, which can quite aptly be called the backbone of the continent. The Sawatch Range stretches for ninety miles from the Eagle River on the north to its southern terminus at Antora Peak, just south of Monarch Pass. This unbroken chain of peaks contains fifteen Fourteeners—the largest group of 14,000-foot peaks in any range in the Lower 48 and the location of the three highest Fourteeners in Colorado: Mt. Elbert, Mt. Massive, and Mt. Harvard. Although the Fourteeners of the Sawatch Range are huge, there's really no risk of falling off the standard route on any of them. I had no reason to suspect that the Sawatch Range would be the site of the most dangerous shoot in my entire Sunrise from the Summit project.

When the spring of 2013 began, I had fourteen Fourteeners to go in my seven-year project. I was determined to finish all fourteen by August, but hoped to do most of them in May and June, when the peaks still held snow. The winter had been dry, but in April a series of massive storms swept through Colorado. By mid-May there was more snow on the high peaks than I had seen at any time of year for several years. I decided to work on Missouri Mountain, Mt. Oxford, and Mt. Belford, a group of peaks that is accessible from a single basecamp high in Missouri Gulch. I planned to shoot the Milky Way from each summit, which meant arriving on the summit at least two hours before sunrise.

The Sawatch Range from the summit of Mt. Shavano
(14,229') at sunrise, San Isabel National Forest.

Looking northwest toward Missouri Mountain (14,067') from the summit
of Mt. Harvard (14,420') at sunrise, Collegiate Peaks Wilderness.

Stormy sunrise over the upper Arkansas Valley from the summit
of Mt. Columbia (14,073'), Collegiate Peaks Wilderness.

It took me five and a half hours to haul a big load of winter camping gear and camera equipment from the trail-head to a high camp at 12,500 feet. Even though it was spring, the temperature on the summit before sunrise would be well below freezing. Hanging out in the cold, wind, and dark for several hours would require plenty of warm clothing. I also needed a winter tent to withstand the potential winds at my exposed camp above timberline, as well as a winter stove setup with enough firepower to melt snow efficiently.

I napped for a few hours in the early evening, then got up again at 10:45 p.m. and began snowshoeing up Missouri Mountain just before midnight. I cached the snowshoes and switched to boots and ice ax when the slope steepened. Two hours after leaving camp, I reached the summit ridge at 13,700 feet. I had never seen such deep, unconsolidated snow on the summit ridge of a Fourteener. High winds normally scour such ridges dry, even in the depths of winter. After two hours of strenuous post-holing along the summit ridge, I finally summited at about 4 a.m., well behind schedule and just minutes before astronomical dawn, the moment when the sky begins to brighten and the stars begin to pale.

I threw on warm clothing and set up the camera as fast as possible. The sky at 14,000 feet on a moonless night still seemed very dark, and the Milky Way glowed against its cobalt background. I managed to shoot a dozen frames before the Milky Way faded into the dawn sky. It was still an hour and a half until sunrise. For an hour I danced and shuffled to stay warm, watching the world below slowly emerge from the gloom of night. Half an hour before sunrise, the second light show began. With the sun still below the horizon, the clouds to the east began lighting up over Mt. Belford, Mt. Harvard, and the valley of Pine Creek. The moment of sunrise was muted as the sun rose into dense clouds, and I headed down soon afterwards, plodding back across the summit ridge, then down the east

King's crown and purple fringe high on the flanks of Mt. Shavano (14,229'), San Isabel National Forest.

face to my snowshoes and eventually to camp. Naturally, I was ready for a long nap, but I still felt strong and healthy. One peak down, two to go!

There are three Fourteeners in Colorado where the only feasible route to the top goes over the summit of an adjacent Fourteener. Mt. Oxford is one of these. Although it wouldn't be necessary to go over the exact summit of nearby Mt. Belford, I would still need to climb to 14,000 feet on the south ridge of Belford, then descend 500 feet to the Belford/Oxford saddle, then gain another 650 feet to the summit

Above: Panorama looking west from the summit of Mt. Elbert (14,433'), San Isabel National Forest.

of Oxford. It had taken me four hours to gain 1,500 feet on Missouri Mountain one day earlier. That's a pace I would have considered pathetic in summer, but in winter-like conditions, with heavy boots and a heavy pack, breaking trail by myself in deep, unconsolidated snow, it was the best I could do. I estimated it would take five and a half hours to reach the summit of Oxford.

I left camp at 10:30 p.m. and summited Oxford at about 4 a.m., almost exactly on schedule. Once again I barely had enough time to shoot a few Milky Way photos before astronomical dawn. Sunrise proved

to be spectacular, with intense color on the clouds to the east and then a deep mauve hue on the clouds over Mt. Elbert to the north and Mt. Belford to the west.

When the sun rose into dense clouds, I headed down. I reached my tent thoroughly exhausted. That afternoon I ate, drank, napped, wrote in my journal, and tried to recover. I didn't have much appetite, but I wasn't feeling sick. I still planned to do Mt. Belford the next day (really, that night), then pack up and hike out. Mt. Belford should be the easiest of the three Fourteeners on this trip, I thought. I had a broken trail to the summit ridge, and from there it was only another 200 vertical feet to the summit. I wanted to summit about 3 a.m. to give myself an hour to shoot the Milky Way, and I figured the climb would take about three and a half hours. I settled in for an after-dinner nap with the alarms inside my hat set for 10:30 p.m.

I left camp at 11:30 p.m. For reasons I did not yet understand, my pace turned out to be much slower than on the two previous ascents. I stopped on top of a knoll at about 13,990 feet when it became clear I wasn't going to make the summit in time to shoot the Milky Way. A large cloud bank was advancing quickly from the south, but I managed to shoot a few frames before the clouds swallowed the stars. I packed up and continued to the summit, where a fierce easterly wind drove me to seek the shelter of a nearby rock outcrop as I waited for sunrise.

Only a few hints of warm light kissed the clouds at sunrise. Slowly I headed back to camp. The day had warmed rapidly and the snow was already soft by the time I reached my tent around

Castle Peak (14,265') and Cathedral Peak from the summit
of La Plata Peak (14,336'), San Isabel National Forest.

10 a.m. Rather than pack up right away and head down, I decided to stay one more night. Instead of battling bottomless slush at midday, I'd get up early, skip any sunrise shooting, and head down on well-frozen snow that would make travel easy. My lack of appetite meant I still had plenty of food and fuel.

The afternoon proved to be quite stormy. The snow anchors I had buried when I first made camp had melted out in the warmth of the previous day. Now they pulled loose. Snow was falling at a rate of an inch an hour. For a time I tried bracing the tent against the powerful gusts, then finally resigned myself to pulling on boots and shells and venturing out into the storm to secure the tent with my ice ax and snowshoes.

Dinner was a packet of freeze-dried eggs, eaten without appetite. Slowly I was realizing that something was wrong beyond mere fatigue and lack of sleep. I developed a cough, but couldn't cough anything up. When I took a deep breath I could feel a faint gurgling in my lungs. The feeling was worse when I lay down, and worse still if I lay on my left side instead of my right. I began to suspect I was developing high-altitude pulmonary edema, a potentially fatal accumulation of fluid in the lungs. I knew my enemy well, since I had developed pulmonary edema at 16,400 feet on Alaska's Mt. Foraker back in 1983.

My condition worsened as the night dragged on. I grew increasingly short of breath. Even rolling over in my sleeping bag made me pant. I got up at 5 a.m., ate a little breakfast, and began to pack. The slightest exertion made me struggle endlessly to catch my breath. I began to count the number of breaths it took me to recover enough to perform the next simple task— first thirty, then forty, then fifty. I thought about sending an SOS on my Spot Connect, an emergency locator beacon that communicates via satellite, but decided I could make it out.

God beams (crepuscular rays) over Twin Lakes and the Mosquito Range as seen from the summit of La Plata Peak (14,336'), San Isabel National Forest.

With everything inside my tent packed up at last, I crawled outside into a cold wind. Digging the tent anchors out of the now-frozen snow took tremendous effort. Finally I had everything stowed in the pack and lashed on outside. Even with most of the food gone, the pack was still heavy, with a camera body, three lenses, a big tripod, multi-row panorama setup, winter tent, warm sleeping bag, hanging stove kit, and on and on.

I made one attempt to hoist my pack, got it as far as my knee, and dropped it. There was no way I could carry that load down 3,000 vertical feet.

I thought about putting the tent up again and waiting for rescue but decided against it. Surely I could walk out under my own power if I didn't have a load. Waiting was likely to make my condition deteriorate still further. I knew that the only sure cure was descent, the farther and faster the better. I took the key to my truck, my wallet, the memory cards from the camera, a pint of Cytomax, a map and compass, and the clothes I was wearing, and started down.

Each step was an effort, but at least I was moving in the right direction, and with each step the air got

Audrey, Glenn, Cora, and Emily Randall on the summit of
Mount of the Holy Cross (14,005'), Holy Cross Wilderness.

Mt. Jackson from the summit of Mount of the Holy
Cross (14,005') at sunrise, Holy Cross Wilderness.

La Plata Peak (14,336') from the summit of Mt. Elbert (14,433') at sunrise
in mid-May, Collegiate Peaks Wilderness, San Isabel National Forest.

a tiny bit thicker. Still fighting for every breath, my mouth and throat grew terribly parched. Every fifteen or twenty minutes I collapsed in the snow to rest. At length I reached an open section of stream and could drink my fill. The snowpack thinned at last and I removed my snowshoes. It took me seven hours to descend 3,000 feet over a distance of three miles and finally reach my truck.

After sleeping in the truck for an hour, I drove home, arriving feverish and exhausted. In the morning I felt better, but was still short of breath. After a few phone calls, I found a mountain guide in Leadville who agreed to retrieve my gear for $250. Fortunately, no one stole the camera gear before he could get to it.

High-altitude pulmonary edema normally strikes people who climb too high too fast. It's fairly uncommon in Colorado, where even the highest peaks are still 4,000 feet lower than Everest basecamp. I had already spent one night at 9,500 feet and three nights at 12,500 feet before I became sick. Did I develop some underlying respiratory infection? I had gotten sick on mountain trips in Colorado before, but never like this. Whatever the cause, I was determined not to let it happen again.

Twilight wedge over the Sawatch Range from the summit
of Mt. Massive (14,421'), Mt. Massive Wilderness.

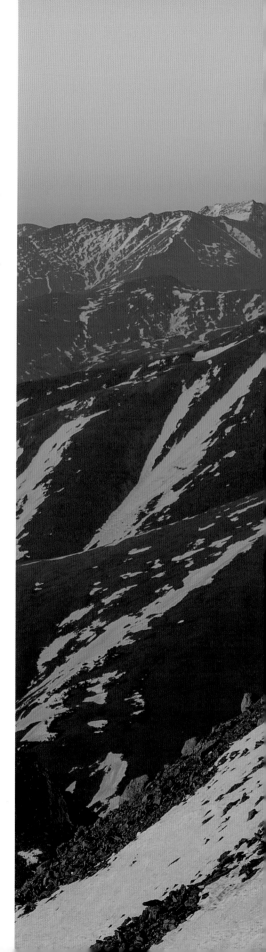

Right: The summit ridge of Mt. Massive and Mt. Elbert (14,433') from the summit of Mt. Massive (14,421') at sunrise, Mt. Massive Wilderness.

When I set out again a month later to do the next five Fourteeners, I gave myself a day off and a night in a hotel in between each peak. The first four shoots went well, and I felt stronger and stronger as the trip progressed. Now it was time to do Huron Peak, the last of the Fourteeners I planned to shoot on that trip. I had already made single-frame shots of interesting portions of the Milky Way from the summit of seven Fourteeners. It was time to up the ante and see if I could shoot a complete Milky Way panorama. The Milky Way occupies an enormous arc as it stretches across the sky from horizon to horizon. It's far bigger, in an angular sense, than any lens can capture in a single frame. Shooting a Milky Way panorama would require shooting multiple overlapping frames, then stitching them together afterwards in software. That, in turn, meant I would need to carry a four-pound panorama head and a heavy tripod, plus my usual eleven-pound camera bag, plus enough food, water, and warm clothing to be comfortable on the summit of a Fourteener all day and well into the night.

The forecast called for clear to partly cloudy skies, with no chance of a thunderstorm. The most recent online trail reports said that a few big lingering snowfields still blocked the trail. By mid-morning, those snowfields would be the consistency of sherbet. I needed to cross them when they were still frozen hard, so I began flexing boot leather around 7 a.m. Fortunately, I had now spent ten days above 10,000 feet, and I was thoroughly acclimated. On Mt. Princeton, at the beginning of the trip, I had barely managed 700 feet of elevation gain per hour and was feeling a bit rocky on the summit. On Huron Peak, despite an even heavier pack, I averaged nearly 1,200 feet per hour and summited in just over three hours.

Now the long wait for sunset began. Photographically speaking, there was little to do until the light became more interesting. Anticipating the wait, I had emailed the notes for my upcoming landscape photography workshop to my phone. Now I whiled away the time delivering my lectures on hyperfocal distance and tilt-shift lenses to the summit cairn, which didn't seem too appreciative of my efforts. A few other mountaineers summited, enjoyed the view for a little while, then began their descent. By 1 p.m. the trickle of other climbers had stopped and I was alone. Thick clouds began to build, which surprised me, given the benign forecast, and I eyed the sky nervously. This was no place to get caught by a thunderstorm.

Lavender sky pilot, Bowl of Tears Lake, and Mount of the Holy Cross (14,005'), Holy Cross Wilderness.

A few strands of virga (wisps of precipitation) fell from the clouds to the south, but no thunderstorm ever threatened Huron Peak. The clouds thinned as sunset approached. The sun found a hole in the clouds just before it dropped below the horizon, and the tips of Ice Mountain and West Apostle began to glow. When the light on those peaks faded, the clouds to the north lit up. In just a few minutes, the light show was over. It was time to wait some more, this time in gathering darkness.

A few minutes before astronomical dusk, I set up the panorama head and began shooting. Each panorama consisted of forty frames in four rows of ten frames each. At first, lingering clouds near the eastern horizon blocked part of the Milky Way. As the night wore on, however, the Milky Way rose above the clouds until it was glowing brilliantly against the near-black sky. I finally declared myself satisfied at midnight and headed down. Two hours later I reached my truck. I slept inside it for five hours, then began the long, caffeine-fueled drive home. ▲▲

Mt. Princeton (14,197') at sunset from the summit
of Mt. Antero (14,269'), San Isabel National Forest.

Milky Way panorama over Missouri Mountain (14,067') and the Sawatch Range from the summit of Huron Peak (14,003'), Collegiate Peaks Wilderness.

Sunrise light on five Fourteeners: Maroon Peak (14,156'), North Maroon Peak (14,014'), Snowmass Mountain (14,092'), Capitol Peak (14,130'), and Pyramid Peak (14,018') from the summit of Castle Peak (14,265'), White River National Forest.

The Elk Range

Capitol Peak, 14,130 feet

Castle Peak, 14,265 feet

Maroon Peak, 14,156 feet

North Maroon Peak, 14,014 feet

Pyramid Peak, 14,018 feet

Snowmass Mountain, 14,092 feet

THE ELK RANGE CONTAINS SIX OF THE MOST beautiful, rugged, and dangerous Fourteeners in Colorado. All of the Fourteeners in the range, and many of the surrounding peaks, are preserved in the Maroon Bells–Snowmass Wilderness, one of the five original Colorado wilderness areas created by the 1964 Wilderness Act. The Elk Range was a fitting choice for inclusion in the fledgling wilderness preservation system. The awesome vistas from the summits of the Elk Range Fourteeners, unlike those from many other Fourteeners, seem to include nothing but wilderness as far as the eye can see.

Only one of the Fourteeners in the Elk Range—Castle Peak—offers a walk-up route. All the others demand serious mountaineering skills. Many veteran climbers regard Capitol Peak as the most technically difficult of all the Fourteeners.

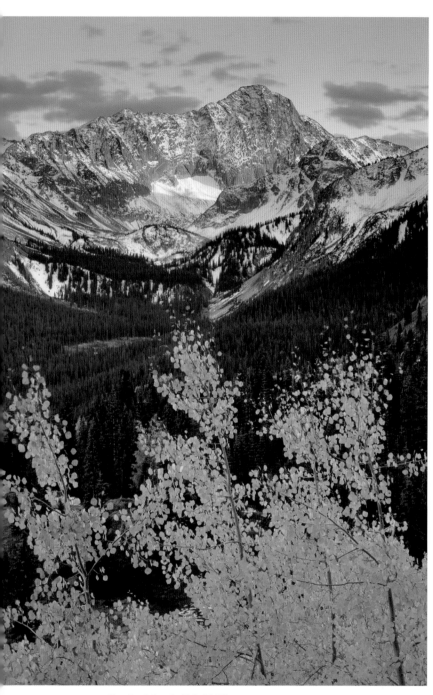

Capitol Peak (14,130') at sunset,
Maroon Bells-Snowmass Wilderness.

That may well be true, although I think that Little Bear, given the conditions in which I climbed it, was significantly harder. Far more intimidating for me than Capitol Peak, however, was the challenge of shooting sunrise from the summit of North Maroon Peak, Maroon Peak, and Pyramid Peak. All three peaks have a well-deserved reputation for long approaches, loose blocks, intricate route-finding, and steep, exposed scrambling. In contrast to Capitol Peak, which is composed of solid granite, Maroon, North Maroon, and Pyramid are made of a crumbling metamorphosed mudstone. The Maroon Bells, as North Maroon and Maroon are known collectively, earned the nickname "The Deadly Bells" after eight climbers died in five separate accidents in 1965. Pyramid, too, has seen its share of accidents, some fatal.

I decided to try North Maroon Peak first. After shooting sunrise at Maroon Lake, I labored up the steep, wet approach route and was delighted to find a tiny but perfect campsite in the highest trees at 11,500 feet. The mid-July weather was flawless, so I decided to scout the route that afternoon, without camera gear. The route proved to be beautiful, with tiny alpine flowers gracing the green patches of tundra. True, the route-finding was intricate and exposed on the summit ridge, but most of the loose blocks had been trundled off the route by generations of passing climbers. I summited in just two and a half hours, descended even faster, and was in bed by 6 p.m. with the alarms set for midnight.

For this climb, I had decided to bring a secret weapon: an old Petzl Zoom headlamp that could throw a usable beam of light 300 feet. True, it was driven by a six-volt battery that lasted only six hours and weighed a third of a pound all by itself.

Right: Collegiate Peaks Wilderness from summit of Castle Peak (14,265'), White River National Forest.

Left: Maroon Bells from Maroon Lake at sunrise.

The weight and short battery life, which made it essential to carry at least one spare battery, had caused me to replace my Zoom years earlier with a lighter, more efficient, but dimmer LED-style headlamp whose beam only penetrated twenty or thirty feet into the surrounding darkness. For this climb, though, I decided that the ability to see farther in difficult terrain was worth the extra weight, so I dug out the Zoom and a couple of old batteries and stowed them in my pack. I did notice that the batteries were years past expiration, but they seemed bright enough when I tested them in a dark room. I figured I might lose an hour or two of battery life, but no more.

Just half an hour into my midnight adventure, however, the first battery died. I had gotten no more than two hours of light from it. I had figured it could take four hours to climb the peak in the dark with full camera gear. If the second battery lasted no longer than the first, I might still be an hour and a half below the summit when I ran out of light. I would miss sunrise for sure, and all my hard work would be for naught.

Pyramid Peak (14,018') and Maroon Bells from Loge Peak at sunrise.

I had timed the trip for full moon, but the moon was hidden behind a high ridge. I tried hiking without the headlamp but kept tripping over unseen roots and rocks. I turned the headlamp back on and turned up my pace. The great headlamp race had begun.

Now my knowledge of the route and daily training regimen paid off. Working hard, I motored up the first gully and traversed on a spectacular catwalk into the second. As the gully steepened, I slowed down

Above: Misty sunrise from the summit of Snowmass Mountain (14,092'), Maroon Bells-Snowmass Wilderness.

and became more methodical. With the headlamp still shining brightly, I was able to relocate the correct route through the cliff bands at the top of the second gully and was soon on the summit ridge. One more crux remained: the steep exit from a 4th-class chimney, but soon it too was below me. I reached the summit two hours and fifty minutes after leaving camp—just twenty minutes longer than it had taken me in daylight with seventeen pounds less camera gear.

I arrived long before sunrise, when only moonlight illuminated the grand spectacle of jagged peaks in every direction. As the sun rose I shot three 360-degree panoramas, then a series of single-frame images of the peaks around me. An hour after sunrise, I reluctantly concluded that I had captured all the good images available that morning and headed down. I had won the great headlamp race. Much more importantly, I had experienced—and photographed—sunrise at the apex of one of the most beautiful wilderness areas in the nation.

I returned a year later to tackle Pyramid Peak and Maroon Peak, which promised to be at least as difficult as North Maroon. For starters, the only reasonable campsite for both peaks is very low, at 10,076 feet at Crater Lake. For most Fourteeners, the highest reasonable campsite is between 11,000 and 11,500 feet. The elevation gain alone—about 4,000 feet—meant that climbing the routes would take a long

Gathering storm over Capitol Peak from the summit of Snowmass Mountain (14,092') at sunrise, Maroon Bells-Snowmass Wilderness.

Snowmass Mountain (14,092') at sunrise from the summit of
Capitol Peak (14,130'), Maroon Bells-Snowmass Wilderness.

Left: Pyramid Peak (14,018') from Maroon Creek Valley, Maroon Bells-Snowmass Wilderness.

time in the dark. When I considered the difficulty of the scrambling and intricacy of the routes, I decided that the only safe way to shoot sunrise from the summit was to climb each peak twice, once in daylight to learn the route, then again the next day by headlamp to shoot sunrise. That meant summiting each peak twice in less than twenty-four hours.

It only took about an hour to hike to my campsite at Crater Lake. That evening, two women from Mountain Rescue Aspen, the local volunteer search and rescue group, walked into my campsite and asked if I'd seen a very tall (six-foot, seven-inch) 190-pound paramedic named Leonard Joyner. He had set off to climb Maroon Peak about four days earlier. No one had seen him since. I told them I'd keep an eye out for him.

My first goal on this trip was Pyramid Peak. I got up at 3 a.m. the next day and was rolling out of camp under a beautiful starry sky just before 4 a.m. I knew the clear sky was deceiving. The forecast called for a sixty percent chance of thunderstorms that afternoon. The summer monsoon had definitely arrived.

As I was laboring up the initial switchbacks around 5 a.m., I saw three headlamps above me, heading down. I soon encountered the lead climber and asked what was going on. "We just saw someone flashing an SOS with their headlamp from North Maroon," he replied. "We're going to hike out and alert the search and rescue team." I told the climbers I admired their selflessness and continued upward.

The sun rose as I crossed the boulder-strewn amphitheater and endured the 800-foot climb on a loose dirt trail to a saddle on the northeast ridge of Pyramid. Now the real scrambling began. With the help of the route description and GPS track from 14ers.com, I found my way up the intricate maze of ledges and cliff bands that forms the upper route and reached the summit four and a half hours after leaving Crater Lake.

During the climb and descent, I saw a helicopter making two round-trips up the Maroon Creek Valley. I hoped it was performing a rescue, but knew it was probably recovering a body. Later that afternoon as I was relaxing in camp, a ranger told me that Leonard Joyner's body had been found. He had succeeded in climbing the south ridge of Maroon and had completed the difficult and dangerous traverse to North Maroon, then fallen at least 500 feet during the descent down North Maroon's northeast ridge. It was a sobering beginning to what proved to be a very intense trip.

That afternoon I ate, napped, then got up again at 11 p.m. feeling like I'd hardly slept at all. The sky was completely cloudy. Maybe, I tried to reassure myself, the evening thunderstorms hadn't yet cleared out.

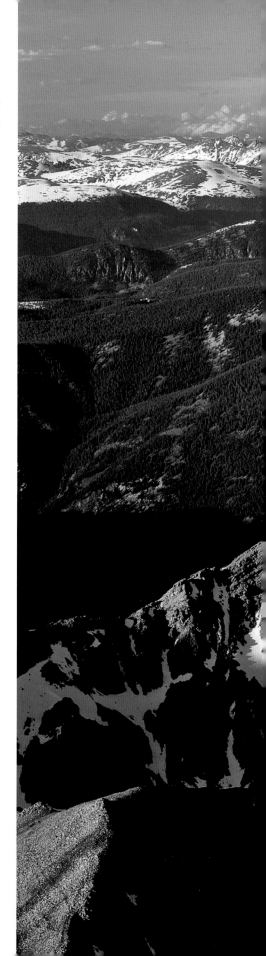

It was, after all, a ridiculously early start. At midnight, just as I was leaving camp, a huge hole opened in the clouds, revealing a brilliant starry sky. Finally it's clearing up, I thought, and headed upward.

Half an hour later, the clouds closed in again, obscuring the summits. A few drops of rain fell. Since there was no thunder or lightning, however, I decided to go to the saddle at 13,000 feet and make the call: up or down. At 3:30 a.m., 100 feet below the saddle, a dense fog suddenly enveloped me. Visibility dropped to fifteen feet as my headlamp beam bounced off the particles of moisture and glared back into my eyes. I continued to the saddle, convinced that I'd just climbed nearly 3,000 vertical feet for nothing.

Once on the saddle, I turned off my headlamp, let my eyes adjust, and scanned the sky. Was there any hope it was going to clear? I still had not seen any lightning or heard any thunder, so there didn't seem to be any immediate danger. Still, it seemed rather unwise to continue up one of the hardest Fourteeners in the state in such dicey weather.

To my surprise, I spotted a couple of stars near the northwest horizon. Then, straining my eyes looking upward, I imagined I saw a star or two straight above. A moment later, the fog dropped below me as suddenly as it had appeared. A thousand stars began glimmering in a moonless sky. I headed upward once again.

I had memorized the key landmarks the day before, as well as created my own GPS route with waypoints at every twist and turn along the way to the summit. With both memory and the GPS to guide me, I was able to stay on the route even in the dark. The stars continued to gleam above me. It looked like my gamble might pay off after all.

One hundred feet below the summit, the fog returned. I summited at 5:15 a.m. in a whiteout. Did I really want to be sitting on top of one of the hardest Fourteeners in the state in such weather? It was still forty-five minutes before sunrise. I pulled on all my warm clothing, wondering if I should descend immediately, and decided against it. It would be easier to find my way in daylight, particularly if the warmth of the sun burned off the fog. I began waiting anxiously.

Gradually it grew light. The fog moved in and out, granting me glimpses of grand vistas one moment, then immersing me in a white void the next. I began shooting. Fog completely filled the East Maroon Creek valley. Periodically it boiled up and swallowed the summit of Pyramid, only to be pushed back by the westerly wind. As the sun rose further, the fog and mist began to dissipate over the Maroon Bells,

Capitol Peak, and Snowmass Mountain. I headed down an hour after sunrise in bright, warm sunshine. Although mist once again capped the Maroon Bells when I finally reached my campsite four hours later, no significant rain fell the entire day. I went to bed early, knowing I still had two back-to-back ascents of Maroon Peak to accomplish.

Above: Panorama of Snowmass Mountain (right, 14,092') and the Maroon Bells-Snowmass Wilderness at sunrise from the summit of Capitol Peak (14,130').

After climbing Pyramid Peak twice in the previous twenty-four hours, I was hardly feeling rested when the alarm went off at 3 a.m. the following day. Despite my fatigue, I was heading toward Maroon Peak just before 4 a.m. I had debated whether or not to bring the camera bag, which weighs about eleven pounds with a body and three lenses, and decided against it. I wanted to move fast, learn the route, and

Left: Wildflowers below the Maroon Bells, Maroon Bells-Snowmass Wilderness.

get down with enough time left to recover before heading out again to climb the peak in the dark and shoot sunrise from the summit.

At the last minute, however, I changed my mind and decided to bring the camera gear. What if I saw some mountain goats, or could grab a few frames of some climbers on the route? What if someone stole my gear as it lay unprotected in my tent?

I hiked fast up the West Maroon Creek trail for two miles, then started up the route on Maroon Peak. For the next three hours, I labored up a steep dirt "trail" that climbs 2,800 vertical feet to a saddle on the south ridge. The useless camera stayed in its chest pack. I finally arrived on the summit five hours after leaving camp without exposing a single frame. After selecting my composition for the next day's sunrise shoot, I headed down.

I was only 150 yards from the summit when I spotted two mountain goats climbing up the same ridge I was descending. The goats continued up to the summit, and I followed. I spent the next hour photographing them on the summit of one of the most spectacular Fourteeners in the state, intensely grateful I had brought the full camera bag. Finally, as the clouds began thickening overhead, I started down for good.

I reached my campsite again at 2 p.m. I estimated it would take me six hours in the dark to climb Maroon Peak, so I set my alarms for 10 p.m. An hour after they jarred me awake I was rolling out of camp again on a clear but moonless night. A strong wind began battering me partway up the east flank of Maroon, but it had eased by the time I reached the summit at 5 a.m. The climb had taken six hours and five minutes.

Soon clouds began lighting up over Pyramid, Cathedral, and Castle Peaks. I used a long lens to make images of ridges stacked up one behind another, then shot two sweeping 180-degree panoramas as the sun came over the horizon. A dense band of threatening clouds was approaching from the west as I headed down an hour and a half after sunrise. A rain shower rolled over me just before I reached my campsite, and more ominous weather loomed over the horizon. I hiked out and pointed the truck toward Boulder, enduring torrential rain all the way from Georgetown to Evergreen. When I finally got home, I checked the point forecast for 13,000 feet on Maroon Peak. It called for an eighty percent chance of rain both day and night for the next several days. I had squeezed in my trip right between two strong surges of the summer monsoon and completed the last two difficult Fourteeners. I had fifteen peaks left, all Class 2 or easier. The end of my epic project, which had already consumed six years, was still a year away, but it was finally in sight. ▲▲

Mt. Wilson (14,246'), Gladstone Peak, and Lizard Head by moonlight from
Black Face, Lizard Head Wilderness, Uncompahgre National Forest.

The San Juan Range

El Diente, 14,159 feet

Handies Peak, 14,048 feet

Mt. Eolus, 14,083 feet

Mt. Sneffels, 14,150 feet

Mt. Wilson, 14,246 feet

Redcloud Peak, 14,034 feet

San Luis Peak, 14,014 feet

Sunlight Peak, 14,059 feet

Sunshine Peak, 14,001 feet

Uncompahgre Peak, 14,309 feet

Wetterhorn Peak, 14,015 feet

Wilson Peak, 14,017 feet

Windom Peak, 14,082 feet

No OTHER RANGE IN COLORADO STIRS THE imagination of the mountaineer and wilderness wanderer quite like the San Juan Mountains. The San Juans sprawl across roughly 10,000 square miles of southwest Colorado—enough jagged peaks, flower-filled valleys, high alpine lakes, and rugged passes for several lifetimes of exploration. The range contains more land above 10,000 feet than any other range in the Lower 48. Several wilderness areas, including the Mount Sneffels Wilderness, the Lizard Head

Wilderness, the Uncompahgre Wilderness, and the Weminuche Wilderness, Colorado's largest, preserve significant sections of the San Juans. Backpackers traversing the ninety-five-mile stretch of the Continental Divide Trail from Stony Pass to Wolf Creek Pass, through the heart of the Weminuche Wilderness, descend below 11,000 feet on only two occasions. The San Juans are home to thirteen Fourteeners, including several of the most challenging Fourteeners in the state.

I began shooting sunrise from the summits of the San Juan Fourteeners in 2006, the very first year of my project, and finished the last one in 2013. Each shoot and each peak has its own story, but several adventures stand out. The first was a winter ascent of Uncompahgre in March 2010.

After my successes in January that year on Quandary Peak and Mt. Elbert, I began wondering if it was feasible to shoot sunrise from the summit of any San Juan Fourteener in winter. Avalanche danger and impossibly long approaches quickly eliminated all of the San Juan Fourteeners but one: Uncompahgre. As the next weather window approached, I saw that it was going to coincide with full moon. When I checked the moon's position in The Photographer's Ephemeris, a very useful mapping program, I saw to my delight that the moon would be setting directly over Wetterhorn Peak, a spectacular Fourteener, at the exact moment of sunrise.

In winter, the road to the Uncompahgre trailhead is plowed only to 9,300 feet. That meant I would have to break trail up 5,000 vertical feet by myself. After spending the night in nearby Lake City, I began hauling my massive mountaineering

El Diente Peak (14,159') at sunrise from the summit of Mt. Wilson (14,246'), San Miguel Mountains, Lizard Head Wilderness.

sled up the snow-covered four-wheel-drive road. The day was gorgeous—so gorgeous I was stopped in my tracks around noon when the fresh snow from the previous day turned to wallpaper paste glued to the bottom of my sled. I scraped off the three-inch-thick layer of ice and snow, but only made it fifty yards before the sled iced up again. I decided to abandon the sled temporarily and break a trail to timberline, still an hour and a half away. When I returned to my sled at 4 p.m., the sun had dropped below the canyon wall and the snow-pack had re-frozen. I spent another hour and a half retracing my steps to timberline, where I camped. It had taken me nine hours to travel four and a half miles and gain 2,500 feet. I turned out the headlamp at 7:30 p.m. and dozed fitfully, questions swirling in my head. Had I set the alarm early enough to reach the summit before sunrise? Would the steep portion of the south ridge be avalanche-prone? Could I find the right gully through the upper rock band in the dark, and, if so, would the snow in the gully be dangerously unstable?

Just four hours and fifteen minutes later, the alarm inside my hat jarred me awake. At 1:15 a.m. I was moving again. Every twenty minutes I stuffed two Clif SHOT Bloks—an endurance food with the consistency of a Gummy Bear—into my cheeks like some two-legged alpine chipmunk. The light of the full moon made my headlamp unnecessary; I turned it off and saw that every snow crystal was sparkling in the moonlight like a highway of diamonds. The night was crisp, with a temperature of about ten degrees and a steady breeze. I broke trail slowly across the vast basin below Uncompahgre, then climbed to the base of the steep portion of the south ridge. Fortunately, I discovered I could hug the ridge crest on a snow-covered

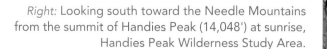

Right: Looking south toward the Needle Mountains from the summit of Handies Peak (14,048') at sunrise, Handies Peak Wilderness Study Area.

Half Mountain at sunrise from the summit of Redcloud Peak (14,034'),
Redcloud Peak Wilderness Study Area, near Lake City.

scree slope and avoid any avalanche danger. I guessed correctly which gully to climb through the steep rock band above and found it filled with shallow powder snow over talus—tedious terrain, to be sure, but not dangerous. With the final obstacle behind me, I panted up the last gentle slope and gained the summit five hours after leaving camp. After shedding my pack and catching my breath, I looked southwest. Wave after wave of snowy peaks extended all the way to Wilson Peak above Telluride. I hadn't seen such a vast expanse of wintery mountains since I summited Mt. McKinley twenty-three years earlier.

With not a minute to spare, I pulled on extra clothing, found my composition, and began shooting a wide panorama as the color of the sunrise light reached its greatest intensity. All too soon, the

Sunshine Peak (14,001') at sunrise from the summit of Redcloud Peak (14,034'), Redcloud Peak Wilderness Study Area, near Lake City.

Mt. Wilson (14,246') from Black Face at sunrise, Lizard Head Wilderness, Uncompahgre National Forest.

moon vanished into the cloud band near the horizon and the color of the light faded to white. I descended slowly to camp, reminding myself in the gully filled with slippery, snow-covered talus that every step mattered. Sprained ankles and blown-out knees were simply unacceptable. Once back in camp, I ate, slept four hours, then wandered around looking for something to shoot at sunrise the next day. Convinced that the now-overcast, lifeless gray skies would never yield a photo that evening, I returned to camp and had just pulled off my boots when the sky exploded into color. I jammed my feet back into my boots without even lacing them and dashed out of the tent, my boots filling with snow. With no time to set up the tripod, I grabbed a few shots handheld as the light peaked, then faded in a matter of seconds. If I had only been disciplined enough to stay outside for another twenty minutes, I would have been able to make a photograph that did justice to the spectacular light.

The next morning I shot a pretty but unremarkable sunrise and broke camp. It took just two and a half hours to stroll back down the trail it had taken nine arduous hours to break two days before.

A year later, the time had come to tackle the three Fourteeners in the Wilson group, which includes Wilson Peak, Mt. Wilson, and El Diente. I decided to try to do all three in one trip and backpacked in to a camp just above Navajo Lake.

I started with Wilson Peak, which taught me, once again, that high-altitude hypoxia and sleep deprivation can lead to such utterly dumb mistakes that it's hard to believe they're even possible. It also taught me that public enemy number one for the wilderness traveler doesn't walk on two legs. But I'm getting ahead of myself.

Moonset over Wetterhorn Peak (14,015') from the summit of Uncompahgre Peak (14,309') at sunrise in early March, Uncompahgre Wilderness

Wilson Peak is a typical San Juan slag heap—awe inspiring when viewed from a distance, but a rubble pile on close inspection. I decided to climb it in late June after an exceptionally heavy snow year to avoid as much slogging on steep, unstable scree and talus as possible.

The next morning I was on the trail at 1 a.m. As I had hoped, I was able to crampon up well-frozen snow for much of the route. The Class 3 section was a bit tricky in the dark, but I arrived on the summit well before sunrise and started shooting as soon as the first glow appeared to the east. When the light

Above: 200-degree panorama looking west at sunrise from the summit of Uncompahgre Peak (14,309'), March 2, 2010, Uncompahgre Wilderness.

show was over, I picked up my pack, looked around carefully to make sure I hadn't left anything behind, and headed down.

Back in camp I napped, read, and ate until it was time for bed. I had already pulled off my boots when I discovered that I hadn't brought my gray headlamp bag into the tent. Annoyed, I pulled on my boots again, climbed out of the tent, and began digging gear out of my pack.

Unease gripped me when I reached the bottom. My headlamp bag wasn't in the pack. I searched my

Right: Jupiter Mountain and Grizzly Peak from the summit of Windom Peak (14,082') at sunrise, Weminuche Wilderness.

tent again. No headlamp bag. Could a marmot have dragged it away? I searched the woods near my tent. No headlamp bag. There was only one other possibility. I had left it somewhere on Wilson Peak, perhaps on the summit and perhaps partway down, where I had stopped to shed clothes.

I debated abandoning it, but that would have meant giving up on any additional sunrise shoots on this trip as well as losing over $100 worth of equipment—the headlamp itself, a tiny backup headlamp, two wristwatch alarms, and more. I decided I had to go back and look, hoping against hope I could find it before someone else carried it off.

The next day I rose at first light and headed up once again. Once I got over the frustration of doing something so stupid, it was actually a rare treat to climb a Fourteener in daylight, after an adequate night's sleep, with no camera gear weighing me down. On the way up, I searched carefully in the area where I'd stopped to change clothes. No headlamp bag.

Summit ridge of Windom Peak (14,082') at sunrise, Weminuche Wilderness.

Left: Twilight wedge over the Needle Mountains from the summit of Sunlight Peak (14,059') at sunrise, Weminuche Wilderness, Colorado. From left to right are Mt. Eolus (14,083'), North Eolus, Turret Peak, Pigeon Peak, and Monitor Peak.

As I approached the summit, I spotted two gray lumps, each the size of a grapefruit, sitting side-by-side. I had to stare hard for several seconds before I realized that one gray lump was a rock; the other gray lump was my headlamp bag. It could not have been more perfectly camouflaged.

The stuff sack had been shredded by some rodent, but the headlamp still worked fine. I headed down, elated. I had one more day of food, so I would still be able to attempt Mt. Wilson the next day. El Diente would have to wait for another trip.

As I approached camp two and a half hours later, I got a shock. My credit cards were strewn across the ground outside my tent. Had some thieving backpacker ransacked my belongings? I unzipped the tent door and saw what had happened. An inquisitive marmot had ripped a hole through the body of the tent, clambered inside, and started chewing. The cash I'd stashed in the tent was scattered about. Fortunately, this marmot apparently preferred laser-printer toner to the scent of greenbacks. He'd taken a single bite from a one-dollar bill and moved on to the letter-size pages I'd printed from an online guidebook. Five full pages had disappeared. Even worse, he'd done some serious chewing on the antenna of my brand-new, state-of-the-art GPS unit, apparently attracted by the odor of the rubbery cladding. He'd then dragged my credit cards outside and abandoned them. Fortunately, the gaping hole in the tent body was under the fly, so no rain could get in.

I looked around for the culprit, but he was gone. Toward evening, as I was settling down in preparation for another truncated night of sleep, I heard a rustling just outside the tent. I looked up to see a marmot—undoubtedly the culprit—poking his nose through the hole in the tent wall. Perhaps he wanted to sample my Thermarest this time around.

"Get out of here!" I shouted, and landed a solid punch on his nose with my fist. The marmot fled instantly and did not return.

When I got home several days later, I spent four hours replacing the mosquito-netting panel in the tent wall that the marmot had gnawed through. Then I bought a replacement for my camouflage-gray headlamp bag. The new one is bright orange.

The imposing north face of Mt. Wilson had compelled my awestruck attention as I stood on the summit of Wilson Peak the day before. Heavy spring snows had left Mt. Wilson's north face covered

with extensive snowfields even though it was late June. In fact, the upper snowfield reminded me of the famous White Spider on the north face of the Eiger. The snowfield ended at the northeast ridge, an airy, 4th-class arête with an intimidating crux just five feet below the summit. Finding my way up that in the dark promised to be a challenge, particularly since I'd never done the route before.

Above: Wilson Peak (14,017') from Last Dollar Road, Uncompahgre National Forest, near Telluride.

The alarm jarred me awake at midnight. By now, the hike up the valley was familiar, even where the trail disappeared beneath the lingering snowfields. Before the trip, I had downloaded a GPS track for the route from 14ers.com. Now it proved quite valuable. I left the valley floor, following the GPS's guidance, and began wandering up the indistinct, rocky buttress that forms the lower half of the route. Sections

Right: Wilson Peak (14,017') and Gladstone Peak at sunrise from the summit of Mt. Wilson (14,246'), San Miguel Mountains, Lizard Head Wilderness.

of easy tundra alternated with broken cliff bands. The GPS guided me toward the easiest breaks in the cliffs.

At the base of the big snowfield, I paused to lash on my crampons and deploy my ice ax. Continuous, ever-steepening snow led me to the northeast ridge. Soon the way up was all too clear: straight up the northeast ridge on delightfully solid rock. Then I reached the crux: an awkward move over infinite air on the right side of the ridge. My big pack, full of heavy camera gear with a tripod lashed on the back, pushed me off-balance. I'd seen a photo of the crux move on 14ers.com that showed a giant handhold. In the dark, that handhold was nowhere to be seen or felt. I looked down again. This was no place to slip. My experience getting offroute on Wetterhorn and Sunlight had taught me one thing: if the way seems too hard, back off. There's probably an easier way.

I retreated a few feet and considered my options. The 14ers.com guidebook had mentioned another way, along the left side of the ridge. This alternate route had a longer section of difficult climbing, but supposedly no single move was as hard. I worked my way along the left side of the ridge for a few feet and picked a new line. It looked feasible—at least as far as my headlamp could reach, about twenty feet. The climbing was steep, but the holds were solid, and there were no off-balance, barn-door moves to negotiate. I emerged onto the small summit just as the first glow appeared to the east. I still had an hour to wait until sunrise.

Soon the light show began. I photographed looking east, then west as the clouds lit up over Kilpacker Basin, then northwest as the red sunrise light hit El Diente, then south as the rugged south ridge of Mt. Wilson caught the light, then finally northeast again as the light from the rising sun reflected off the east-facing cliffs below me and bounced a warm glow onto the shadowed sides of the towers jutting up from Mt. Wilson's northeast ridge. Those glowing pinnacles (shown at right), combined with the spectacular sight of Gladstone Peak and Wilson Peak jutting up against the dawn sky, make this photograph one of my all-time favorite Sunrise from the Summit images. ▲▲

Following page: Full moon rising over the Mosquito Range, seen from the summit of Mt. Elbert (14,433') in January, San Isabel National Forest.